SUE SMITH has been writing for television for nearly thirty years. Her television credits include *The Young Doctors*, *The Leaving of Liverpool*, *Brides of Christ*, *Bordertown* (the last three co-written with John Alsop), *The Road from Coorain*, *R.A.N. Remote Area Nurse*, *My Brother Jack*, *Temptation* and *The Cooks*. Her feature film, *Peaches*, was produced in 2003, and her first stage play, *Thrall*, was performed at the Old Fitzroy Theatre in 2006.

The war on the wharves.

BASTARD BOYS

Sue Smith

Currency Press,
Sydney

First published in 2007 by
Currency Press Ltd
PO Box 2287, Strawberry Hills NSW 2012 Australia
enquiries@currency.com.au
www.currency.com.au
Reprinted 2015

NATIONAL LIBRARY OF AUSTRALIA CIP DATA
Smith, Sue, 1959- .
Bastard boys : the screenplay.
ISBN 9780868198095 (pbk.).
1. Bastard boys (Television program). 2. Television mini-series - Australia. 3. Television plays, Australian. 4. Strikes and lockouts - Stevedores - Australia - Drama. I. Title.
791.45720994

Cover photographs from the ABC TV drama, Bastard Boys, reproduced courtesy of ABC TV. Photographs by John Tsiavis and Gary Johnston. Cover design by Kate Florance, Currency Press.

All photographs that appear in this publication are from the ABC TV drama, Bastard Boys, and are reproduced courtesy of ABC TV. Photographers: John Tsiavis and Gary Johnston.

Printed by SOS print+media, Alexandria, NSW.

CONTENTS

MAIN CAST AND CREW

John Coombs
Colin Friels

Chris Corrigan
Geoff Morrell

Greg Combet
Daniel Frederiksen

Sean Mcswain
Anthony Hayes

Josh Bornstein
Justin Smith

Julian Burnside
Rhys Muldoon

Brendan Tully
Daniel Wyllie

Janine McSwain
Justine Clarke

Petra Hilsen
Lucy Bell

Tali Bernard
Caroline Craig

and Jack Thompson
as Tony Tully

Directed by
Ray Quint

Produced by
Brett Popplewell and
Ray Quint

Written by
Sue Smith

Executive Producers
Miranda Dear and
Scott Meek

Director Of Photography
Louis Irving A.C.S.

Production Designer
Paddy Reardon

Editor
Veronika Jenet A.S.E.

Costume Designer
Marion Boyce

Composer
Jan Preston

The Producers gratefully acknowledge *Waterfront: The Battle That Changed Australia* by Anne Davies and Helen Trinca

On April 7th, 1998, war broke out on the Australian waterfront between Patrick Stevedores and the Maritime Union of Australia when Patrick dismissed its entire unionised workforce. It was a war that would change the nation.

Greg's war: Greg Combet (Daniel Frederiksen) addressing the wharfies.

SCENE 1. EXT. PATRICK'S MELBOURNE DOCK. NIGHT.

Melbourne. Opening credits over a series of shots of the waterfront in operation on a chilly autumn night. The lights. The huge ships in dock. The rows and rows of stacked containers. Forklifts and straddle carriers in motion. The huge, bright red cranes, emblazoned in bold blue and yellow with a single word: 'PATRICK'.

Super caption: 'April 7th, 1998'.

SCENE 2. INT./EXT. STRADDLE CARRIER – PATRICK'S MELBOURNE DOCK. NIGHT.

High up in a crane, emblazoned with the white P & O sign, a wharfie punches a number into a mobile phone.

In a straddle carrier on the Patrick dock, Tony Tully, late 50s, answers his mobile.

TONY: Tommo? I'm up for a beer if you are.

P & O WHARFIE: Tone. There's something going on. There's dozens of blokes in boats coming up the river. They've got uniforms. And dogs.

TONY: Dogs?

P & O WHARFIE: Yeah, mate, and they're not flamin' poodles.

TONY: Uh. So you don't reckon they're planning a barbie, then?

SCENE 3. INT. LIMBO. DAY.

Brendan Tully, 27, addresses the camera.

BRENDAN: Where was I when it happened? I was in Number Three crane. Been hanging out for Number Three for months –

then this. Never been so scared in my life. Dead set, I shat myself.

Super caption: 'Brendan Tully, Wharfie'.

SCENE 4. INT./EXT. CRANE – PATRICK'S MELBOURNE DOCK. NIGHT.

Brendan is looking down from his seat in a crane, watching as literally dozens of security men in white shirts, black pants, ties and peaked caps fan rapidly, in disciplined formation, across the dock. Many have large dogs on leashes.

BRENDAN: Fuuuck ...:

And he's barely gathered his wits when he sees, appearing at the top of the ladder to his crane cabin, a security man.

SECURITY MAN 1: Get down, please. You're no longer employed by this company. Give me the keys to the crane.

BRENDAN: What?

SECURITY MAN 1: Give me the keys.

SCENE 5. INT. LIMBO. DAY.

Tony Tully, 58, addresses the camera.

TONY: Me? I was in a straddle.

Super caption: 'Tony Tully, Wharfie'.

SCENE 6. EXT. STRADDLE CARRIER – PATRICK'S MELBOURNE DOCK. NIGHT.

Tony talks into the walkie-talkie connection on his straddle.

TONY: Hey, Legs. There's a bloke down here with a cute little puppy.

A large security man with an immense, black Rottweiler.

I think I might kill 'em.

He hurls the straddle into gear and begins to drive it straight towards the security man, who narrowly avoids being run down. The Rottweiler barks in fear.

SCENE 7. INT. LIMBO. DAY.

John Coombs, 57, addresses the camera.

COOMBS: Do? What could I do? They rang on the mobile. I'm dead to the world down on the farm. In the caravan with Gwen. I went back to sleep. Think it was the last time for a year.

Super caption: 'John Coombs, National Secretary, Maritime Union of Australia'.

SCENE 8. INT. LIMBO. DAY.

Sean McSwain, 35, addresses the camera.

SEAN: Lying awake. Thinking about Janine. When I got down there, I thought: 'Man, this is the closest I ever want to get to a war'. I've never seen anything like it. Never thought I would see anything like it. Not in this country.

Super caption: 'Sean McSwain, official, MUA'.

SCENE 9. EXT. PATRICK'S MELBOURNE DOCK. NIGHT.

Chaos on the docks. Rapid cuts. Frightened and angry wharfies are running this way and that, calling out to each other, being chased by security guards with dogs. Tony Tully shouts to the men.

TONY: Get to the amenities room. Just get to the amenities room and we'll find out what's going on.

Security Man 1 addresses a man in a forklift.

SECURITY MAN 1: I insist you climb down and give me the keys to the vehicle. I repeat: you are no longer employed.

Straddle cranes are racing among the stacks of containers like long-legged spiders. Security men and dogs scatter in all directions. The wharfies driving the straddles communicate with each other through their walkie-talkies. They look crazed under the night-lights. The straddles move at dangerous speed amongst and around the containers.

Some images are seen as though through security cameras: high angles, low angles. A couple of times the image fragments as a straddle carrier runs over and smashes the camera.

Tony has bailed up the supervisor and is shaking him by the collar.

TONY: You don't expect me to believe that! You're the flaming supervisor. How can you not know?

A dog barks at the camera. Frightened, aggressive.

SCENE 10. INT. LIMBO. DAY.

Greg Combet, 39, addresses the camera.

COMBET: The first thing I did? Listen to Hendrix. I went to school in Rooty Hill. Y'had to psyche yourself up to face the sharpies somehow. Dogs, for Christ's sake. In every port in the country. What sort of evil genius thinks of something like that?

Super caption: 'Greg Combet, Assistant Secretary, ACTU'.

SCENE 11. INT. LIMBO. DAY.

Chris Corrigan addresses the camera.

CORRIGAN: I was asleep. No one believes me. They say how can you mastermind something like that and then sleep through it? But I was. Dreaming, actually. About this mad old Hungarian refugee I worked for as a kid. Employed a lot of the local kids – we were cheap, of course. And he'd get us out in his market garden at three am in the bloody Mittagong winter, freezing, cutting the bloody celery. And he used to say 'Work a little harder, bastard boys'. Never forget it. 'Come on, bastard boys. Work harder.'

Super caption: 'Chris Corrigan, Managing Director, Patrick Stevedores'.

And bring up title:

BASTARD BOYS

PART ONE: GREG'S WAR

Super caption: 'Six months earlier'.

SCENE 12. EXT. MAIN GATE – WEBB DOCK. DAY.

John Coombs presents his MUA pass to the security man at the gate to the Patrick dock. The security man grins.

PATRICK SECURITY MAN 1: G'day, Coombsie. Out to call a stoppage, are you, mate?

COOMBS: Mate, if I was to call a stoppage, it'd be your lucky day. (*'You'd'*) Make twice your yearly salary in one day, scabbing.

He grins and goes through as Security Man 1 switches on a walkie-talkie.

PATRICK SECURITY MAN 1: Union coming through. The Greyhound.

VOICE: (*on the walkie-talkie*) Greyhound?

PATRICK SECURITY MAN 1: Coombsie. 'Cos he makes a little white hair go a long, long way.

Muffled laughter from the walkie-talkie. Coombs, without turning back, raises his middle finger in the air. He heard.

SCENE 13. INT. THE AMENITIES ROOM – PATRICK'S MELBOURNE DOCK. DAY.

A small group of wharfies are having their lunch, and chiacking each other over their MUA voting forms. Among them are Tony and Brendan Tully. Sean McSwain is there, too, but is only half joining in the fun. His head is buried in a book.

Coombs walks in.

COOMBS: All right, you lot, you're sprung. Rumour up in management that you've been nicking the brass taps again.

General welcoming response from the men. Much back slapping and good-natured embracing. Coombs is a popular figure.

TONY: (*indicating the name 'Sean McSwain' on the form, and gesturing to Sean*) Just in time, mate. We're sticking pins in the voting form for the elections. Reckon young Mac here deserves a go?

COOMBS: ... Well, they say we get the officials we deserve. I reckon you lot of ugly mugs deserve Sean.

Sean looks up from his book and grins.

SEAN: Endorsed by the man himself.

TONY: Coombsie, meet my boy, Brendan. Just come on as a casual.

COOMBS: Good to meet you.

BRENDAN: Likewise. Hey, can the Union do something about the billiard table? Been asking them for a week to replace the felt, and nothing's happened. The old man thought we might call a national stoppage over it.

He grins at his father, taking the piss.

COOMBS: I've called 'em for less, mate. Hey, where's Podge? He's not still crook?

BRENDAN: He's on the nick.

COOMBS: I didn't hear that. (*To Sean*) You didn't hear it either.

BRENDAN: That's right, mate. Once you become a union man you get selective amnesia.

SEAN: (*grinning*) What's 'the nick'?

Good-natured laughter from everyone.

SCENE 14. INT. THE AMENITIES ROOM – PATRICK'S MELBOURNE DOCK. DAY.

Coombs and Sean have moved away from the others and are finishing a cup of coffee.

SEAN: Management still on about crane rates?

COOMBS: Mate, if Chris Corrigan had his way, you blokes'd be up in those cranes for seven hours straight, eating your lunch with one hand, driving the crane with the other and using the opposable big toe on your left foot to hold your todger while you piss in a bottle. How're things at home?

SEAN: Pretty good. You know.

Coombs gives him a look: don't lie to me, son.

Same. She's staying at her mum's. I saw the kids on the weekend, but she wouldn't come out of the house.

COOMBS: You ever want some of Gwen's famous lasag, the door's open. Can give you a decent feed at least.

SEAN: Thanks.

Coombs gives him an encouraging pat on the shoulder, puts his empty cup down and makes his way out.

SCENE 15. EXT. DOCKS. DAY.

Various shots of the waterfront in action. Wharfies operating cranes. The cranes lifting the containers from the ship's deck, then lowering them to the ground to be lifted by the straddle carriers in their turn.

A sense of the actual business of the waterfront.

REITH: (*voice over*) ... The Australian waterfront is an international joke. We are laughably behind world's best practice. We should be achieving crane rates of twenty-five container movements per hour, and instead we're at a miserable fifteen ...

SCENE 16. INT./EXT. COOMBS' CAR – STREET. EVENING.

Sydney. Coombs is driving home from the airport, listening to PM. *It is the continuation of the interview with Peter Reith, Federal Minister for Workplace Relations.*

REITH: (*on the radio*) ... Our wharfies get paid seventy-five thousand dollars a year for working eight hours a week. Talk about lifestyles of the rich and infamous. In a globalised, competitive marketplace this is a sick joke ...

SCENE 17. INT. AN OFFICE. DAY.

A male figure in a suit moves behind a partition in a large, busy bureaucratic office. His face remains hidden.

Well-kept fingers dial a number on a telephone.

SCENE 18. INT./EXT. COOMBS' CAR – STREET AND DRIVEWAY. EVENING.

Coombs' mobile phone is ringing. Coombs, still not entirely comfortable with the thing, feels in his jacket pockets, on the seat, in his trouser pockets …

COOMBS: Struth … Hello?

FRIEND NUMBER 1: Is that John Coombs?

COOMBS: Yes. Who's this?

FRIEND NUMBER 1: A friend. Are you on your own? Can you talk?

COOMBS: I can talk.

FRIEND NUMBER 1: Okay. Listen carefully. I'm calling from Canberra. The shit's about to hit the fan.

Coombs rapidly executes a one-handed, lopsided turn into his driveway. The front garden bed takes a bit of damage.

COOMBS: I'm listening.

FRIEND NUMBER 1: First thing: stay off the fixed phones. They've got them tapped. Just speak digital to digital. Get a copy of the Army newspaper. There's a recruitment ad in there. They're going to bust you. They're going to bring in military people to take over the waterfront. They're going to train people in Dubai.

Coombs is sitting in the car in his driveway. Gwen comes out to see what's keeping him. Coombs mouths to Gwen.

COOMBS: Got a live one here. (*Into the phone*) Who? Who's doing all this? Why are you telling me this?

FRIEND NUMBER 1: To be honest, I think you lot are your own worst enemies. But this is beyond the pale. I've gotta go. I'll call when I can, but things are …

The connection is terminated. Coombs looks to Gwen.

COOMBS: Made a new friend, Gwennie.

SCENE 19. EXT. ARMY RECRUITMENT CENTRE. DAY.

John Coombs stands outside the Army Recruitment Centre in the middle of the city, and goes in.

SCENE 20. INT. ARMY RECRUITMENT CENTRE. DAY.

Coombs looks around at the recruitment posters on the walls with puzzlement and mild distaste. Images of focussed and determined young, fit military types. Not up his alley at all. He finds the Army magazine, picks it up and begins to casually browse through it. Until he finds, in a centre page, a recruitment ad seeking trade specialists to work in a surface transport area.

SCENE 21. EXT. MUA. DAY.

Coombs crosses Sussex Street and turns into the head offices of the Maritime Union of Australia. He bounds up the front steps encountering a young official as he does so. He slaps the young man heartily on the back …

COOMBS: How're you settling in, mate? Okay?

… And doesn't wait for an answer. The Army magazine is under his arm. He is clearly distracted.

SCENE 22. INT. RECEPTION AND COOMBS' OFFICE – MUA. DAY.

Coombs walks from the lift into the office. His mobile is ringing.

COOMBS: Hello?

FRIEND NUMBER 1: Did you see it?

COOMBS: Wait a moment, will you?

He makes his way rapidly into the office, past the receptionist who's holding out a sheaf of messages for him. He ignores them, moves as though in a dream past several others and into his own office, pushing the door firmly shut.

They're wharf jobs. Gotta be.

FRIEND NUMBER 1: Got the passports through in five minutes flat. They're smoothing the way for serving soldiers to go as well.

COOMBS: How far up does it go?

FRIEND NUMBER 1: How far do you want to go?

COOMBS: Let's start at the top.

FRIEND NUMBER 1: Well, you can start with the PM.

COOMBS: Howard? Howard's in this?

FRIEND NUMBER 1: From Howard down. Listen, I can't call any more. People can hear me ... I'll pass you on to someone else. Talk to him. He knows a lot.

The call is disconnected. Coombs just sits. He is pale.

COOMBS: Jesus ...

A union official, Mick, sticks his head in the door.

MICK: You coming to this credit-union meeting, Johnno?

COOMBS: Yeah, mate, yeah. There in a tick.

Mick goes. Coombs lays the army recruitment ad on his desk in front of him. And just sits. Completely poleaxed.

SCENE 23. INT. SYDNEY TOWN HALL. NIGHT.

The Town Hall foyer. A large sign announces that tonight's lecture is by Neville Wran on the subject of Australia becoming a republic. The foyer is full of Labor Party members who have attended the lecture. They cluster in small groups, sipping wine and chatting.

John Coombs makes his way through the throng, slapping a back here, shaking a hand there. It's clear he is a well-known, respected and popular figure. And finally, he sees his quarry: the tall, dark, bespectacled figure of Greg Combet. Combet spies

Coombs, smiles and excuses himself from the group of people he's with. He and Coombs hug.

COOMBS: Worst bloody day of my life the day Bill Kelty poached you. (*To the assembled*) My protégé here. Look at this get-up. You iron your shirts these days, do you, Greg?

COMBET: Foreman material, brother. Got to get your priorities right.

COOMBS: Not one of his shirts so much as sniffed a bloody iron when he worked for me.

He puts an arm around Combet's waist and draws him away. Physically they are a very odd couple: Combet a tall, youthful Clark Kent; Coombs small and nuggetty, blue eyed, white haired. A bantam.

Can we get out of this chardonnay-swilling mob and talk?

COMBET: Thought you were growing chardonnay down the farm.

COOMBS: No, mate. Pinot.

They disappear into the throng.

SCENE 24. INT./EXT. COOMBS' CAR – MILLERS POINT. NIGHT.

Combet in the passenger seat, Coombs the driver. The car is parked high up in Millers Point, above the docks at Darling Harbour.

By the car interior light Combet studies the Army recruitment ad.

COMBET: From Howard down?

COOMBS: I knew they were coming for us, but I never thought they'd resort to bastardry like this.

He climbs out of the car and goes to lean on the railing, looking down over Darling Harbour. Combet follows him. From here, they can see the big red Patrick cranes.

COMBET: If you want to smash the union you've got to find an alternative workforce. They couldn't train a scab workforce anywhere in the country without us knowing about it. So they're going offshore. Is it Corrigan? It's the sort of stunt he'd pull.

COOMBS: Wouldn't know a good pinot if it fucked him.

Combet laughs. But he's thinking it through, rapidly, rationally.

COMBET: ... Say it is an existing operator. Say it is Corrigan. Once you've got two workforces, what do you do with the one you've already got?

The full implications of this thing are beginning to dawn on both men.

COOMBS: So we've got a government up to its neck in a plot to throw two thousand legitimately employed taxpayers out of a job?

It's too wild a proposition to take seriously.

COMBET: Nah. Whoever it is, even if they wanted to, they couldn't get round the unfair-dismissal regs.

COOMBS: They play silly-buggers with me, I'll close the whole place down. Month before Christmas. Pull out every port in the country.

COMBET: I don't think that's the way to go, John.

COOMBS: What?

COMBET: We've got to be smarter than that.

He starts to pace, thinking hard. Using the expletive as though it is a tool of logic.

Fuck fuck fuck fuck fuck fuck fuck fuck fuck ...

COOMBS: Always admired your capacity for disciplined thought, Greg.

COMBET: Mate, that was disciplined thought. We've got to get this into Parliament. Ambush the bastards.

COOMBS: You're the only person I've told. 'Cept Gwennie. I haven't even told my own officials.

Combet nods, aware of this statement of trust.

I can't fight this on my own. We're too small. I need the ACTU.

COMBET: John, you're going to need the whole bloody labour movement. And then some.
COOMBS: But have I got you?

A sudden, unexpected and quickly hidden flash of vulnerability.

COMBET: You need to ask?

SCENE 25. INT./EXT. – COOMBS' CAR – STREET. DAY.

Next morning. Coombs is driving towards the city from his Roselands home when his mobile rings. He looks at it. No number.

COOMBS: John Coombs.
FRIEND NUMBER 2: I've got some documents that might interest you.
COOMBS: Go on …

SCENE 26. INT. HOTEL ROOM. DAY.

Combet is hurriedly trying to bolt down a piece of toast and a cup of hotel instant coffee and iron his shirt at the same time. Two broadsheet newspapers are scattered all over the bed and the morning radio news is on. His mobile is ringing.

COMBET: John …
COOMBS: You sitting down?
COMBET: I'm ironing my shirt, actually.

Coombs laughs.

COOMBS: You're a cool customer, I'll give you that. I've had another call. Not the usual bloke. It's getting too hot for him, he says. I'm calling this one 'Friend Number Two'. You ready for this? He told me to get someone up to the Ettamogah Pub in Queensland. Says he's got documents that'll bring down the government …
COMBET: The Ettamogah? Not that fuckin' sticky-floored tourist joint on the Sunshine Coast? Ten bucks a beer. Mate, whoever this mob is, they're all class.

SCENE 27. INT. COOMBS' OFFICE – MUA. DAY.

An MUA secretary hands a priority parcel to Coombs. Coombs and Combet, alone in Coombs' office, rip the parcel open and begin poring through the contents. On the letterhead of Fynwest Pty Ltd is a standard letter and a contract.

COMBET: They're contracts. Highly confidential. Training programme … Dubai Port Authority … Accommodation in Dubai covered, major credit cards accepted … Jesus.

Among the documents are CVs of the two principals of Fynwest Pty Ltd. There are photographs of Mike Wells and Peter Kilfoyle with details of their backgrounds. Both have a background in the Special Air Services.

They're goons.

He's on his feet. Pacing. Thinking.

Who's got the skills to operate heavy machinery? Who's tough enough to handle it if there's biffo from the union? The military. It's Corrigan. It's gotta be. Rapacious fuckin' merchant banker.

A wry smile on Coombs' face.

COOMBS: Guess who's got the Super Fund Christmas lunch?

COMBET: There's not much time, John. This says they're flying on the third. That's five days.

SCENE 28. INT. THE BOARDROOM – MUA. DAY.

The final board meeting for the year of the union superannuation fund. In attendance are John Coombs, Chris Corrigan and several other board members.

COOMBS: So, all business being done, I declare the meeting closed at one fifteen p.m. And I suggest we repair to Edna's Table where they're holding our usual table.

CORRIGAN: (*standing, gathering papers, minutes etcetera*) In the corner so the good working folk of Sydney don't see you lot consorting with the enemy.

Coombs falls into step beside Corrigan.

COOMBS: So, how's business, Chris?

CORRIGAN: You tell me. Have a look at my share price. You lot are sending me broke. Might sell up on the waterfront and …

COOMBS: … And dedicate yourself to philanthropy?

CORRIGAN: I was going to say, 'sell up on the waterfront and go back to my first love'.

SCENE 29. INT. EDNA'S TABLE RESTAURANT. DAY.

The group around a large table, drinking red wine as their food is delivered. Coombs and Corrigan are seated side by side, talking. There's a buzz of conversation from the others. Coombs is watching Corrigan like a hawk, looking for any small sign of another agenda.

CORRIGAN: Chickens … Good pinot. You socialists know a good drop when you sniff one. I bred chickens as a kid. Sold them to the local butcher in Mittagong three years in a row.

COOMBS: Good little earner?

CORRIGAN: Not bad. I used to caponise them – you know, de-sex them so they'd get plumper. Trouble is, they discovered the drug I was using got into humans and started de-sexing them as well. Not an entirely bad thing in the population of Mittagong, in hindsight.

Despite his innate suspicion of Corrigan, Coombs bursts out laughing.

SCENE 30. EXT. SUSSEX STREET. DAY.

Coombs walks along Sussex Street back to the MUA office, his teeth just slightly stained from red wine, talking into his mobile.

COOMBS: Cool as a cuke, mate. Not a slip.

SCENE 31. INT. SYDNEY AIRPORT. DAY.

Combet sprints on his long legs towards the departure gate for a flight to Melbourne. He is talking into his mobile phone.

COMBET: Yeah, well, he's hardly going to say 'Fair cop I dunnit', is he? How was the pinot?

Combet thrusts his boarding pass into the attendant's hands.

COMBET: (*still into the phone*) We need to co-ordinate media coverage of these goons flying out to Dubai with springing the trap in question time …

SCENE 32. INT./EXT. COMBET'S CAR – ANNA'S SCHOOL. EVENING.

Melbourne. Combet is still on the phone as his car pulls up beside the school.

COMBET: … There's a block booking from Melbourne to Dubai on the third. It's got a high-level security classification …

He's out of the car, running now.

… There's a leak from the Defence Department. Same stuff – soldiers training in Dubai …

SCENE 33. INT. THE AFTERCARE CENTRE – ANNA'S SCHOOL. EVENING.

Combet is still on the phone as he hurries in to aftercare. Waves to Cecilia, the Islander childcare worker, and leans down to sign his daughter, Anna, out.

COOMBS: (*over the phone*) … I've got two words for you mate. 'Daffy Duck'.

The phone is still glued to his ear as his daughter, Anna, 6, comes towards him. He lifts her and hugs her with one arm, the other still clenching the phone to his ear.

COMBET: (*to Anna*) Hey, sweetie… (*Into the phone*) *'Daffy Duck'?!*

SCENE 34. INT. THE HALLWAY AND LIVING ROOM – COMBET'S HOUSE. NIGHT.

Combet swings open the front door. He's carrying his own overnight bag plus a bag of Anna's clothes. Anna follows him in. She walks with a slight limp, her feet turned in from birth. Television sounds come from the living room.

COMBET: Petra's got your room all ready for you. You take this down and I'll organise some dinner.

Anna takes her bag from him and begins to move off. Combet watches her walk.

Anna. Are those insoles still hurting?

ANNA: A bit.

Combet makes his way towards the living room, Anna hovering beside him. She is clearly shy and feeling out of place.

Sitting in the living room watching the television are Clara, Combet's thirteen-year-old stepdaughter, and Yannis, his five-year-old stepson.

COMBET: Hi, you two.

YANNIS: Hi, Greg.

No answer from Clara. He didn't really expect one.

COMBET: Where's your mum, Clara?

CLARA: (*'How dare you speak to me?'*) I dunno.

Blended families …

SCENE 35. INT. THE LIVING ROOM – COMBET'S HOUSE. NIGHT.

Anna sits on one side of Greg and Yannis on the other, both kids in their pyjamas, as he reads to them from a Tintin comic.

He likes Tintin, and he loves the kids, but tonight his mind is elsewhere.

COMBET: '"It looks like … It looks like a huge ball of fire." "Yes, Tintin, it's a gigantic mass of matter in fusion, heading towards us at an incredible speed." "But if it keeps on coming?" "Yes, that fireball is going to collide with the earth!" "Great heavens, but that'll mean ... the end of the world." "Yes!"'

Greg's partner, Petra, comes in, trying not to interrupt. She carries shopping bags in one hand and a pile of files in the other – everything about her says 'busy working mother'. She might have the merest trace of a German accent.

PETRA: Hi kids. Sorry I'm late. Welcome home.

She drops a kiss on Greg's head and tousles the heads of the two kids. Greg reaches over his shoulder, takes her hand, and continues.

COMBET: '"I've finished the calculations. The collision will take place tomorrow morning at oh-eight-twelve hours and thirty seconds precisely ..."'

SCENE 36. INT. THE BEDROOM – COMBET'S HOUSE. NIGHT.

Greg and Petra lie quietly in bed, Greg stroking her hair.

COMBET: D'you know, when I first went to the MUA they had to have a special vote of the national executive. 'How can we contemplate polluting the ranks with this wetback? Never lifted a wharfie's hook in his life. He's an *acafuckingdemic*, for God's sake.' This union will fight to the last man for its traditions – always has. It's why the Libs want to smash it. They know they only need to get non-union blokes in one port in the country and we're dead. And I look at John Coombs –

SCENE 37. INT. THE BATHROOM – COOMBS' HOUSE. NIGHT.

Combet's voice continues over as John and Gwen Coombs finish dressing their son Garry, 36, after his bath, and help him ease back into his wheelchair. Garry has MS. They exchange comments: 'Easy, easy' ... 'Watch your back' etcetera.

Above: Greg Combet and his family. Left to right, Anna Combet (Joanna Hunt-Prokhovnik), Greg Combet (Daniel Frederiksen), Petra Hilsen (Lucy Bell) and Yannis Hilsen (Kurtis Papadinis). Below: security on the wharf.

COMBET: (*voice over*) – Started working at fourteen. It's all he's ever done. And this jockey-sized whippet and his intermediate certificate are the only things standing between that tradition and total annihilation.

SCENE 38. INT. THE BEDROOM, HALLWAY AND KITCHEN – COOMBS' HOUSE. NIGHT.

Coombs is half asleep, restless. The bedside radio is on. He stirs, finding a familiar voice penetrating his consciousness.

GWEN: (*on the radio*) I'm married to a wharfie, Ian. I've been married to him for thirty years.

IAN: (*on the radio*) What's your name, darling?

GWEN: (*on the radio*) Gwen.

IAN: (*on the radio*) Well, Gwen, you're on a pretty good wicket, aren't you, love? He's only at work a few hours a week, then comes home with a monster pay packet – if he hasn't blown it in the pub on the boss's time, that is.

Coombs gets out of bed and walks down the hall towards the kitchen. There is Gwen, red-faced with anger, talking into the phone.

GWEN: You're wrong, Ian. You're as wrong as wrong as can be. The wharfies I know are good, loyal, kind blokes. They do their jobs. They love their kids. And whatever they get paid, they deserve more. And you are a pea-brained stooge for a government full of card-carrying ... Baptists.

She looks up to see Coombs standing in the doorway. Smiling.

Black screen.

Super caption: 'December 3rd, 1997'.

SCENE 39. INT. COMBET'S OFFICE – ACTU. DAY.

Combet is straightening his tie, smoothing his hair, cleaning his glasses, as Coombs comes in. Coombs is nervy, Combet icily calm and focussed.

COOMBS: In there, waiting to pounce. Wait 'til your tongue's stuck to the roof of your mouth like a stale communion wafer, then they pounce.

COMBET: I'm not Catholic.

SCENE 40. INT. THE BOARDROOM – ACTU. DAY.

The middle of a press conference: reporters with cameras, mikes, tape recorders. All humming with the anticipation of something big. Combet ceremoniously looks at his watch.

COMBET: It's ten past two. At just about this moment, thirty-six either former or serving Australian military officers are waiting to board a plane for the United Arab Emirates. There they'll be joined shortly by a second group and the entire contingent will be trained, in absolute secrecy, but with the full knowledge and co-operation of the Federal Government, to take up jobs on the waterfront.

He takes a sip of water. His mouth is dry. Despite his apparent calm, he is not yet confident about his ability to handle the media. Coombs, on the other hand, uses the adrenalin of the moment to turn himself into something of a showman, using his closed fist on the table to emphasise his points.

COOMBS: Our sources are rock solid, ladies and gents. If you don't believe me, call the Travel Lodge out at Tullamarine and say the word 'Daffy Duck'. I kid you not – that's the password. It'll get you straight through to them. This government is allowing its serving officers to be used as industrial mercenaries to launch an unprecedented and relentless assault on a legitimate trade union.

There's some uproar in the room.

JOURNALIST 1: How do you know the government's involved?

JOURNALIST 2: Who's tipped you off?

JOURNALIST 3: Who in the government knows about this?

JOURNALIST 4: What's your source?

JOURNALIST 5: Is Chris Corrigan involved?

Several other journos punch out numbers on their mobile phones and murmur into them: 'Daffy Duck' ... 'Daffy Duck' ... 'Hello, is that the Travelodge? Daffy Duck'.

Combet tries hard to stifle his grin.

COMBET: (*sotto voce*) 'Industrial mercenaries'. You fuckin' beauty.

SCENE 41. TELEVISION NEWS FOOTAGE.

News footage.

FEMALE ABC JOURNALIST: (*voice over*) ... Still in doubt whether the men are to take up jobs off shore, or, as is more likely, as strikebreakers in Australian ports. Assuming the latter, the men have been described by the union as industrial mercenaries ...

A group of men try to avoid news cameras as they file through the departure lounge at Tullamarine airport. They are all identified by their short military-style haircuts, but that is the only apparent similarity: the men are 'in disguise'. Some wear suits and carry newspapers and briefcases, some wear board shorts and loud Hawaiian shirts. Some wear jeans and carry backpacks. All of them stick out like a collection of sore thumbs.

News footage of Question Time in Parliament House, Canberra. The opposition leader, Kim Beazley, questions the Prime Minister, John Howard. Lindsay Tanner, shadow Workplace Relations Spokesman, hurls questions at the government benches.

SCENE 42. INT. THE BAR – A MELBOURNE CITY PUB. NIGHT.

Sean, alone and bleary eyed, gulping down the most recent of several beers, watches the news on the television above the bar.

SCENE 43. INT. THE LIVING ROOM – COOMBS' HOUSE. NIGHT.

Coombs, Gwen and Garry watch the late news. Gwen is ironing John's shirt.

SCENE 44. INT. COMBET'S OFFICE – ACTU. NIGHT.

Combet is sitting in front of the television, close, watching and then rewinding an interview with Chris Corrigan. Perhaps the programme is Lateline *and the interviewer Tony Jones.*

CORRIGAN: I think I'm on record as having admitted frustration at the pace of waterfront reform. We've been trying to negotiate with the union for months on the issue of productivity increases and, frankly, it's like we're stuck in quicksand.

ABC INTERVIEWER: And do you think your company would ever get involved in something like this? Employing sort-of ex commandos, ex army, military types in order to break a strike is the essential allegation of the Opposition.

CORRIGAN: It's just so hypothetical a proposition, I can't – I can't respond to it. I mean it's the first I've heard of the circumstance. I'm not sure I understand what is being proposed.

Combet watches Corrigan's face, looking into his videotaped eyes, rewinding, over and over … 'I can't – I can't respond to it …

COMBET: (*whispering*) You're lying, Chris.

There's a similarity between the two men – one older, one younger – a similar razor-sharp intelligence, a similar level of focus and zealotry about their cause. Combet continues to stare at Corrigan, trying to peer into the soul of his nemesis.

SCENE 45. INT./EXT. THE BACKYARD AND LIVING ROOM – COMBET'S HOUSE. NIGHT.

Combet walks across his backyard towards a large cage, which houses roughly 30 or so Gouldian finches – rare Australian native birds. He climbs into the cage, replaces the birdseed and the water. All this as he listens to Coombs on the mobile.

COOMBS: Round one to us, mate.

COMBET: We're running a marathon, John. Not a sprint.

COOMBS: Are you in that flaming birdcage again?

COMBET: They sell for thirty bucks a pop, you know. Rare species. They're my retirement plan if the bum ever falls out of the labour movement.

COOMBS: 'Retirement plan' my arse. You even think about retiring on me, brother, and I'll …

He can't think of anything. And so he hangs up.

Combet rings off, and looks through the rear glass doors into the living area of the house. And smiles. He moves quietly inside. Petra has fallen asleep, pen still in her hand, over scattered pages of a budget for the East Melbourne Childcare Centre. He lifts the pen from her hand, puts it down, and gently smooths a strand of her hair from her face as she begins to stir.

SCENE 46. INT. COMBET'S OFFICE – ACTU. DAY.

Greg Combet's office at the ACTU. The walls are covered in graphs and a large whiteboard features with flow charts of ACTU policy. Elsewhere are posters for various ACTU campaigns: work safety, women in the workplace, universal superannuation, childcare, Medicare, indigenous rights, May Day rallies. In pride of place is a labelled photograph of Combet's mentor, Tas Bull, signed 'To Greg …'

At first audible, then visible on a television, is news footage of Bill Kelty's rousing speech at the 1997 ACTU conference.

KELTY: To weaken the Maritime Union of Australia is to weaken the union movement as a whole. The day we give away that support is the day we rip out our own heart and leave it pumping in irrelevancy ... The only promise to John Howard is this: 'If you seek to destroy the Maritime Union of Australia, we will be there, and you won't have a picket of thirty people, or a picket of forty people. You won't have a picket of five hundred people. You will have the biggest picket that has ever been assembled in this country ...'

Combet, at work, watches the speech on video. He looks up as a figure appears in the doorway behind him. Bill Kelty. In the flesh.

Not bad, uh?

SCENE 47. INT. KELTY'S OFFICE – ACTU. DAY.

Kelty and Combet, boss and junior, with the choreography and body language that relationship implies.

KELTY: So. How d'you want to run this?

COMBET: Uh ...

KELTY: It's your union. I'm going to let you run it. Assuming you want to.

Combet's rare grin splits his face.

COMBET: Fucking oath I want to run it. I'm itching to run it.

KELTY: Can you work with Coombsie? He's not like you, y'know. He's old-school. You're all head, he's all heart.

COMBET: I can work with him. He might take a bit of persuading on tactics, but I'll get him there.

Kelty looks at his protégé for some moments, assessing the faint arrogance implicit in his manner.

KELTY: You're a bit of an ambitious young dick, aren't you, Greg?

COMBET: Never denied it.

KELTY: You know you're considered next in line for my job? You're seen as the most promising young official in years.

Combet is silent. Kelty watches him, assessing.

You do want this job, don't you?

COMBET: Yeah. I want it. But I don't know if I can do it.

KELTY: No. Course you can't. You're not ready. That's what I told your fan club.

COMBET: It's never gone to anyone from the Left before.

KELTY: They'll vote the way I tell 'em to vote. But you're not ready. I'll let you run this one. You make the calls, I'll support you. But this is big. The government's going to chuck everything they've got at us. Stuff up, the other unions'll drop like chokos off the shithouse wall. Get us out of this one alive, Greg. Do that, and this job might still exist when you're ready for it.

SCENE 48. INT. A CORRIDOR – ACTU. DAY.

Combet walks out of Kelty's office, closing the door behind him. He stops for a moment, absorbing the weight and the meaning of the previous scene, pulls his glasses off, pinches the bridge of his nose. And stands completely still.

A moment, then he springs back to focus, replaces his glasses, and moves off.

SCENE 49. INT. THE LIVING ROOM – COMBET'S HOUSE. NIGHT.

In the background Clara does the washing up as Yannis and Anna watch a kids' movie on tape.

All three are out of earshot of Combet and Petra at the dinner table.

COMBET: Bill more or less anointed me today as his successor.

PETRA: Well. You want it, don't you?

COMBET: I'd lose a limb for it.

PETRA: But? It's a poisoned chalice?

COMBET: Union membership non-compulsory and in decline. Legislation that makes industrial action almost impossible. The most stridently anti-union government in history. Yep. It's Camelot. And I'd lose a limb for it.

Petra smiles, teasing him.

PETRA: Tonight I'll read you *Das Kapital*. In the original. All right?

COMBET: Getting hard just thinking about it.

The smile between them: secret, sexy, very much in love. But, safe with Petra, Greg allows his vulnerability to show.

I'm the class nerd, pet. I learned my negotiation skills trying to stop the sharpies sticking my head down the dunny. If I fuck this thing up, we're toast.

PETRA: Then don't fuck it up. (*To the kids*) Hey, you two. Five minutes, then bed.

SCENE 50. INT. THE BOARDROOM – MUA DAY.

Gwen Coombs looks on, trying to hide her obvious amusement, as a slightly flustered John Coombs is given media-handling lessons by Jane Singleton.

SINGLETON: Don't lick your lips. You look shifty. And look straight down the barrel. Okay. What's your response to allegations of rorts on the waterfront?

Coombs instantly licks his lips.

No lips.

COOMBS: The productivity increases they're demanding are pie in the sky. They can't be achieved with outdated equipment …

SINGLETON: Hands. Watch the hands. No. Not that. You looked away. I wouldn't believe a word you said.

SCENE 51. INT. THE BEDROOM – COOMBS' HOUSE. NIGHT.

Coombs is in bed, in his pyjamas. Gwen potters around putting on face cream. Coombs is practising.

COOMBS: Productivity. Is that the only word left in the English language? What about safety? Because that's what the three-for-two work practice is about. Three drivers, two cranes.

Continuous operation, sensible meal breaks, work spells that are efficient and safe. *You* spend eight hours straight driving a straddle with your head doing a one-eighty to your body, and see how you feel.

GWEN: You pointed.

COOMBS: What?

GWEN: You pointed.

COOMBS: I did not point.

GWEN: Don't point. It's threatening. And 'three-for-two's using arcane language.

COOMBS: Don't point. Don't lick lips. Keep it simple and stare down the barrel. Anything else?

GWEN: Keep your jacket on. The viewers don't like sweat stains.

And the shittier he gets the funnier she finds it.

SCENE 52. INT. A CONFERENCE HALL. DAY.

Coombs appears to still be practising. Until it's revealed he is wearing a suit, and lit by a spotlight, and standing at a lectern facing an (unseen) audience. It's the International Transport Federation Conference. He struggles not to lick his lips or wave his hands. He stares right down the barrel of the camera. And he is every inch a statesman.

COOMBS: And so I come to London today to ask for your help. The International Transport Federation is one of the most powerful international labour movements in the world. The Maritime Union of Australia is a tiny union with a huge history and an even bigger heart. Right now our tiny, proud union needs your muscle. Stop these scabs being trained offshore. Threaten to close down the Port of Dubai. No scabs on the waterfront. In Sydney, Melbourne, Fremantle. Dubai. Or any port in the world.

Applause. No need to reveal the audience.

SCENE 53. INT. CRANE – PATRICK'S MELBOURNE DOCK. NIGHT.

Melbourne. Sean McSwain is in his crane, working the twilight shift. He is talking on his mobile phone to his wife, Janine.

SEAN: ... Couple of hours OT ... Well, we didn't make any arrangement for the weekend, and I um ... Oh, hell, the soccer camp. Forgot the shitting, bastard soccer camp ...

He pulls a hipflask from his pocket and takes a hefty slug. From the redness of his eyes this is not his first drink of the evening.

SCENE 54. INT. THE BEDROOM – COMBET'S HOUSE. NIGHT.

A mobile phone is ringing. It's four a.m. Greg Combet puts out a sleepy hand towards the phone.

COMBET: Hello?

He is greeted with loud party noise and an exuberant and rather pissed John Coombs.

COOMBS: Merry Christmas, Comrade. London calling.

COMBET: John ...

COOMBS: We nailed 'em, Greggie. The Federation leaned on the Ambassador for the Arab Emirates over Assam tea and cucumber fuckin' sandwiches. 'The scabs go or there won't be a single container across your docks.' They cancelled their visas. Within twenty-four hours.

Combet is starting to smile.

You should've seen his face, mate. It was a beautiful thing. Cucumber sanger half-in, half-out.

COMBET: (*catching Petra's eye, grinning*) Have you been drinking, John?

COOMBS: No, mate, it's jetlag. I'm at the ITF Christmas party, for crying out loud. Is the Pope Polish?

COMBET: Keep telling you: I'm not Catholic.

COOMBS: Yeah, well, you might want to think about converting.

In the background, at the party, Combet can hear a rousing chorus of 'Solidarity Forever'.

Solidarity forever, Greg, mate.

COMBET: Solidarity forever, brother.

And down the phone, the delightfully pissed Coombs starts singing 'Solidarity Forever'. Combet just laughs, and even finds himself mouthing the words. He holds the phone so Petra can hear. Four a.m., Melbourne, and the two are sitting up in bed listening – and pretty close to singing along with – a workers' anthem sung by a drunken man halfway across the world.

SCENE 55. EXT. PATRICK'S MELBOURNE DOCK. NIGHT.

Brendan has knocked off his shift and is walking from his straddle carrier past the cranes when he looks up to see Sean lose his footing on the crane ladder and slide the remaining few yards, landing in a crumpled heap at the bottom.

BRENDAN: Shit! You alright, Mac?

He reaches Sean to find that he is physically unharmed but very drunk.

Mate. You smell like a brewery. Have you worked a whole shift in this state?

SEAN: Liquid lunch …

Brendan looks around in case there's a supervisor nearby.

BRENDAN: Come on. Outta here. Quick.

He hauls Sean to his feet, and half carries him away.

SCENE 56. INT. THE KITCHEN – TULLYS' HOUSE. NIGHT.

Sean is sitting slumped at the kitchen table. A near antique chamber pot sits on his lap. A bed-tousled and half-asleep Tony Tully busies himself making bacon and eggs while Brendan fiddles with the kitchen radio, trying to tune it to something worth listening to. After a while he finds the news.

TONY: Not happy, Mac. Not freaken happy, son.

Sean stares dully at the tabletop.

How long's this been going on?

SEAN: Since she left.

TONY: Oh, and you'd be the first bloke in the world whose missus done a flit, huh? Listen, son. You are standing for election to the best union in the country. You've got a tradition to uphold. You're following the Jim Healys and the Tas Bulls. They'd be turning in their graves.

BRENDAN: If they were dead …

TONY: I bloody *voted* for you.

SEAN: Backed the wrong horse, then, didn'ya? I'm a social leper, didn't you know? I can empty a room in five minutes flat.

TONY: Look at yourself. What's wrong with this picture, huh? And you wonder why she left … The only thing right with this picture is me poor bloody sainted Nan's bloody chamber pot. And God knows, that's seen better days.

The news is burbling away, but now Brendan turns it up.

NEWSREADER: … In a victory for the Maritime Union the United Arab Emirates has denied entry visas for what the union described as 'industrial mercenaries'. After tense discussions with representatives of the International Transport Federation and the MUA, the UAR …

Tony's wife Lyn staggers in, hair awry, face creased from sleep.

LYN: What's this? Some sort of corroboree?

SCENE 57. INT. CORRIGAN'S OFFICE – PATRICK HEAD OFFICE. DAY.

Sydney, very early morning. Chris Corrigan walks into his office pulling his motorcycle helmet off. As he pulls out the earplugs of his transistor radio the broadcast becomes audible.

NEWSREADER: ... Chose to withdraw the visas rather than face retaliatory action from the ITF in its principal port of Dubai. The men were to take part in a training programme on the Dubai docks, which the union alleges was designed to equip them for a possible strikebreaking role here in Australia ...

Corrigan sits at the desk, listening, and quietly taps a pencil on a notepad.

SCENE 58. INT. RECEPTION – PETER REITH'S OFFICE. DAY.

Canberra. A sign on the door: 'The Honourable Peter Reith, Federal Member for Flinders'.

Greg Combet sits, waiting, one long leg crossed over the other. He's nervous and trying to hide it. Glances at his watch.

Coombs, flustered, hurries in.

COOMBS: Sorry, sorry, sorry. Bloody Qantas ...

Combet smiles at the receptionist.

COMBET: Just give us a moment, would you?

He speaks quietly to Coombs.

Whatever happens, we stay cool, okay?

SCENE 59. INT. PETER REITH'S OFFICE. DAY.

Peter Reith – big, stocky, balding. Tough and arrogant. The Federal Minister for Workplace Relations.

REITH: For the umpteenth time, I know nothing about training a workforce in Dubai or anywhere else. But if someone wanted to, would you blame them? You blokes have been lying, cheating, rorting and ripping off the system for decades.

COMBET: If this is about three-for-two, it's the only way to ensure continuous operation. Stop it, and the whole port shuts down for meal breaks. What'll that do to your productivity rate?

REITH: Three-for-two's an excuse for the nick and you know it.

COMBET: Look, you won't hear me or John defending the nick.

But you can't expect John in an office in Sussex Street to control what happens at Fremantle. If it's happening, it's up to the port managers to stop it –

Coombs' fist thumps down on the table in what is his traditional emotional negotiating technique.

COOMBS: I dunno what bloody Corrigan's telling you, but we've been trying to work with him for a year. We offered him a productivity bonus – the blokes who get their rates up get a bonus. Simple. Turned up his nose like we'd put a dead rat on his cornflakes. And I'm stuffed if I'll subject my blokes to neck injuries just to …

REITH: (*interrupting*) A bandaid to fix cancer. That's what you offered. You're dinosaurs, you people. You know that, don't you? What are you going to do when the farmers finally get jack of their exports sitting on the docks, rotting? What are you going to do when they come marching down from the bush and take over your jobs? Mmm?

And Mr Calm and Rational loses it.

COMBET: You lying germ. You piece of scum.

COOMBS: Greg …

COMBET: You pig-ignorant also-ran suburban fucking abacus. How much's the big end of town paying your election fund, huh? What are you getting out of wedging the community apart? Destroying the working wage? Denying workers their democratic right to protest? It's fun, isn't it, laughing up your smug suburban lawyer sleeve while you chuck honest people out of jobs.

REITH: I think the meeting is over …

COMBET: We're going to fight you. We're going to fight you with every weapon we've got – and you know we've got 'em, you spineless grub. And if that scares you, why don't you ask your mate the PM nicely, he might buy you a backbone for your next birthday. It's probably too fucking late to buy you a conscience.

Reith stands and leaves the room. Absolute silence. Combet slowly slides back into his chair. His face is ashen, his hands shaking.

COOMBS: You know, Greg, I've always admired your capacity for disciplined thought.

SCENE 60. INT. RECEPTION – PETER REITH'S OFFICE. DAY.

Coombs and Combet emerge into the foyer. There, facing them, is a media scrum of cameras and microphones. Combet is still white as a ghost.

COMBET: Oh, Jesus ...

COOMBS: Bit of advice, son. Don't point. Stare down the barrel. And use words the mums and dads can understand.

And they breathe deeply as they walk forward into the camera lights.

SCENE 61. INT. THE LIVING ROOM – COMBET'S HOUSE. NIGHT.

Coombs and Gwen are dining with Combet and Petra.

COMBET: That can't happen again. Can. Not. Happen again.

COOMBS: I didn't know you had it in you, mate. I'm proud of you.

COMBET: What'd I call him?

COOMBS: A 'pig-ignorant also-ran suburban effing abacus'. Never forget it.

COMBET: Oh, Jesus.

In truth, he's pretty ashamed of losing it so badly with Reith.

Tomorrow with Corrigan we've got to play it smarter.

COOMBS: Listen, if Chris Corrigan gets on my wick, I'll shut him down. It brought him to heel last time. He knows I'll do it.

COMBET: We can't play it like that anymore, John. The legislation's changed. We call a stoppage and they'll fine us out of existence.

COOMBS: So what do you suggest? 'We'll fight you with every weapon we've got'; what weapons've we got left if we can't strike?

And here is the nub of the conundrum. Combet's reluctant to admit it, but knows he must.

COMBET: I don't know. That's the trouble.

Coombs opens his mouth to reply, but Combet knows it's now or never.

COMBET: But I know the old days are gone. The old hairy-chested stuff won't work anymore. Yeah, we controlled the waterfront. Once. Not now. We can't out-muscle them. We've got to outmanoeuvre them.

COOMBS: You saying my record's stuck?

Tension. Apparently out of nowhere.

COMBET: I'm saying we're operating in a completely new legal and industrial environment. We've got to find a different way.

COOMBS: You keep saying that. But what? What?

GWEN: How's Anna, Greg?

COMBET: She's all right. I think. We're still doing the week-about thing.

PETRA: At least in this house they've all got a bit more space –

Coombs ignores the women's attempt to head off the conflict.

COOMBS: Maybe I'm stuck in a rut? Past it? Because I can't see a new and different way falling from the sky.

COMBET: I didn't say …

COOMBS: Excuse me. Bathroom that way?

PETRA: Third on the right.

Coombs heads down the hall, bumping into Clara as she appears from the hallway.

COOMBS: Sorry, love …

An awkward moment.

PETRA: Clar?

CLARA: Mum, you have to sign Yannis' excursion form.

Petra stands and begins to move off, Clara following.

CLARA: (*generally*) Um. Good night.

GWEN: Goodnight.

COMBET: Night, Clara.

The answer 'Night, Greg' doesn't come. Combet meets Gwen's eye for a moment and looks away.

GWEN: (*sotto voce*) It'll pass.

Combet nods. This stepfather thing is tough.

There's life in John yet, you know.

COMBET: And I'm an overeducated dickhead, right?

Gwen lets that go right through to the keeper.

GWEN: I do like the new house ...

Combet starts, and then that all too rare smile takes over his face and he laughs.

SCENE 62. INT. CORRIGAN'S OFFICE – PATRICK HEAD OFFICE. DAY.

Sydney. Chris Corrigan faces Coombs and Combet.

The office is high above Kent Street, with a view down to the docks at Darling Harbour. An enormous floor-to-ceiling world map takes up one wall.

COMBET: We want to know if you were involved in Dubai.

CORRIGAN: Does it matter? It's collapsed now, hasn't it?

COMBET: Were you involved?

CORRIGAN: No.

COMBET: Because if you were, everything we've offered is off the table.

CORRIGAN: I didn't hear you offer to stop your members working half a shift and then nicking off to the pub on full pay. I didn't hear you offering to stop them snoozing up in the crane for an entire shift so we'd be forced to give them overtime.

COOMBS: I talked for an entire day in Melbourne to get that last enterprise agreement up.

CORRIGAN: Yes – and your men have thumbed their nose at it. They're not abiding by it at Webb dock, and you know it. And what about the Sydney Branch? They're completely out of control.

They do know it.

COMBET: We want to know what you're planning.

CORRIGAN: What I'm planning? I'll tell you what I want. If that helps. I want to be able to look my shareholders in the eye and tell them they can trust me. I want the people who work for me to do a decent day's work for a decent day's pay. That workforce – down there – is miserable. Not because they're exploited, even though that's what you'd have them believe. But because of archaic work practices, inefficiencies, enforced delays, ridiculous convoluted chains of command. Because imposed mediocrity forces them to go home every single day of their working lives knowing they haven't done their best. People want to take pride in their work. I want them to be able to. But you won't let them.

COMBET: I think we all agree motherhood's a wonderful thing. We want to know what you're planning.

CORRIGAN: I'll tell you the other thing I want. I want this company to start turning a profit. I realise that's a dirty word to a socialist. In fact, let's test just what good socialists you are.

Leaning back in his chair, a gleam of mischief in his eyes.

I'll sell you the company. For a dollar. I'll even give you the dollar.

He pulls out his wallet and plonks a dollar coin on the table.

It's going broke, of course. But maybe if you own it, you'll be able to change things. There it is. Genuine offer. Patrick, the Australian stevedore, going for a dollar. Take it or leave it.

Silence for some moments. Coombs and Combet stare at the coin, both trying to hold their tempers. Corrigan watches them, cat-and-mouse style.

Finally, Coombs' fist thumps onto the table.

COOMBS: Chris, for Christ's sake, stop talking shit, and just tell us what the fuck's going on.

CORRIGAN: Ah, well. You'll just have to wait and see, won't you?

SCENE 63. INT. A LIFT – PATRICK HEAD OFFICE. DAY.

The lift doors open and Coombs and Combet walk in, both slightly stunned.

COOMBS: We're dead. He's in it up to his neck.

COMBET: I've got to pick up Anna.

SCENE 64. EXT. CITY STREET. DAY.

It has been raining. Cars splash the two men as they speed past. One taxi passes. Combet tries to hail it. A second. A third. All full. A rainy late afternoon two days before Christmas. Chaos.

COMBET: Shit …

COOMBS: What's the rush?

COMBET: I've got to get Anna from day-care by six.

COOMBS: Well, isn't there someone …

COMBET: No. There isn't 'someone'. We don't all have wives that stay at home …

He breaks off before he can go any further. Coombs sees his level of distress, and leaves it alone.

Coombs hails a cab on the other side of the street.

COOMBS: There. Quick. Go. Go.

Combet rushes through the traffic to the other side of the road, opens the cab door, and calls out to Coombs, through the traffic.

COMBET: I'll get some polling done. Focus groups.

He climbs into the cab.

COOMBS: (*calling back*) What?

COMBET: Focus groups …

The cab pulls away.

COOMBS: Focus … what?

SCENE 65. INT. THE DEPARTURE LOUNGE – SYDNEY AIRPORT. DAY.

Combet is pacing in the packed airport departure lounge talking anxiously into his mobile.

COMBET: Pet, I know you're stuck in the conference. My flight's delayed. If the traffic's bad in Melbourne I won't get to Anna in time. If you get this message ... What? I dunno what I expect you to do about it. Sorry. I'll call in when I land ...

Under this, a Qantas announcement:

ANNOUNCER: Ladies and gentlemen, we apologise for the delay. We should be boarding in just a few more minutes. Thank you for flying Qantas, and thanks for your patience.

Combet glances at his watch again. Oh, shit ...

SCENE 66. EXT. THE AFTERCARE CENTRE – ANNA'S SCHOOL. EVENING.

It has been raining in Melbourne too. Combet sprints through the schoolyard, breathless, his feet splashing through puddles. And hurls himself into the open door of the centre.

SCENE 67. INT. THE AFTERCARE CENTRE – ANNA'S SCHOOL. EVENING.

COMBET: Anna?

The centre looks empty.

Cecilia?

Now Cecilia appears, Anna following. Both wear red-and-white Santa hats. Combet goes down on his knees and hugs Anna.

I'm so, so sorry I'm late, sweetheart. Are you okay?

Anna nods her head. Combet exhales, gets his breath back.

CECILIA: I called her mum. She said it was your week.

Ouch.

COMBET: Thanks for waiting, Cecilia. I appreciate it.
CECILIA: No worries, Mr Combet. Hey. Merry Christmas.

SCENE 68. EXT. THE AFTERCARE CENTRE – ANNA'S SCHOOL. EVENING.

Greg opens an umbrella for Anna.

COMBET: I'm really sorry, Anna.
ANNA: You said that.
COMBET: It's ... important stuff at work. You know.

She doesn't reply. How can he explain it to a six-year-old?

Hop on.

He crouches down and lets her get onto his back. And she promptly plonks her Santa hat on his head. Combet piggybacks her across the yard, Anna holding the umbrella high to protect them both. As they move away from us:

Hey, it was raining in Sydney too.
ANNA: I know. Sydney has higher rainfall than Melbourne, but Melbourne has a higher proportion of rainy days.

She's a chip off the old block.

COMBET: Is that right?

The very tall, umbrella-waving pair walks off, one of them with a Santa hat slipping down over his glasses. Gradually they disappear into the grey of the coming evening.

SCENE 69. INT. COOMBS' OFFICE – MUA. DAY.

Sydney. Coombs swings into his office waving a scrap of paper. He is trailed by Mick, one of his officials.

COOMBS: Leak from the Construction Union. Someone wants to hire cranes for use on the Melbourne waterfront. Message was to call Paul ...

Coombs speed dials the number.

G'day, is that Paul? ... Yeah. Heard you were looking to

hire some cranes? ... Name's Eric ... Yeah ... Yeah, we can do that, no worries at all. But, listen, mate, is the wharfies' union okay about this? They're a pack of mongrels ... It's sweet? Good-oh ... And you're from? ... National Farmers' Federation. Goodonyoumate. I really admire what you fellas stand for ...

His eyes connecting with Mick's as he puts his hand over the mouthpiece of the phone.

MICK: You gunna tell us what's going on, John?

COOMBS: On a need-to-know basis, brother. On a need-to-know basis.

SCENE 70. EXT. MAIN GATE – WEBB DOCK. DAY.

Peter Kilfoyle appears at the security gate and shows his pass.

KILFOYLE: Name's Kilfoyle. Here to install some security at Webb Number Five.

PATRICK SECURITY MAN 1: We expecting a war or something?

KILFOYLE: (*smirking*) Something.

SCENE 71. INT. THE LIVING ROOM – COMBET'S HOUSE. NIGHT.

On the television David Hardaker is breaking a story on the ABC's 7.30 Report.

HARDAKER: With the Dubai scheme now a thing of the past, the Maritime Union has had time to take a breath over Christmas. But their troubles are far from over. Tonight we reveal a new plan to bust the monopoly of the union. This time it's run out of the offices of the National Farmer's Federation ...

Combet stares open-mouthed at the screen.

COMBET: Fuck. It *is* the farmers ...

SCENE 72. EXT. WEBB DOCK. DAY.

The morning shift finishes off.

Super caption: 'January 28th, 1998'.

The buzzer goes for shift changeover. Tony Tully climbs down from his straddle and looks around, wondering where his replacement is.

TONY: Where is everybody?

He walks across to where Brendan and Chopper are muttering to each other.

Hey, wake up, dreamy drawers. You're on.

BRENDAN: Mate, I've just broken the land speed record getting here, and Captain Hook's telling me to bugger off ... No shift.

CHOPPER: Twilight's cancelled, apparently.

TONY: No shift?

BRENDAN: Yeah. No shit.

Tony looks puzzled. And then suspicious.

TONY: What's going on?

SCENE 73. INT. THE LIVING ROOM – SEAN'S HOUSE. DAY.

Sean looks on as his five-year-old son, Alex, unwraps a Christmas present. His mother, Sean's wife Janine, emerges from another room carrying bags of clothes for herself and the children.

ALEX: Mum! It's a Play Station.

SEAN: There's a couple of games too. Maybe we could have a game before you go back to school. I've missed you, mate.

JANINE: You shouldn't've done that, Sean. It's too much.

Sean shrugs.

SEAN: Let's set it up, eh?

JANINE: Isn't it better if we take it back to Mum's?

SEAN: Well, do you want me to set it up there, or what?

JANINE: Um. Look, I'd rather you didn't ... Mum's ... we'd just ... rather you take Alex out and stuff ...

Sean looks completely winded. One blow after another.

SEAN: I haven't seen him since before Christmas. That's a whole month, and you won't even bloody let me ...

His mobile phone is ringing.

Shit shit shit shit shit ... What?

COOMBS: (*on the phone*) You better get down to Webb Dock, mate. Pronto. There's been a lockout.

SEAN: What? Why?

COOMBS: (*on the phone*) 'Cos you're the union rep. Didn't they tell you? You won the vote.

Sean absorbs this for a moment, and then he starts to laugh.

SEAN: You're kidding me, Coombsie, aren't you?

COOMBS: (*on the phone*) No violence. Whatever happens, Mac. No violence.

Sean hangs up. Still laughing.

SEAN: You're looking at the new MUA state official.

JANINE: That's kind of funny.

SEAN: Oh yeah? Why?

JANINE: Unions are about people, Sean.

SCENE 74. EXT. MAIN GATE – WEBB DOCK. DAY.

A row of immense men in blue overalls and caps stands in a row by the front gate, arms folded across their chests. They are huge, disciplined, unintimidated by the cluster of angry and abusive workers outside the gate.

SCENE 75. INT. THE AMENITIES ROOM – PATRICK'S MELBOURNE DOCK. DAY.

A group of thirty or so wharfies is holed up in the amenities room, Tony and Brendan Tully among them. Tony is shouting down the stairs.

TONY: You tell those bastards we're not going anywhere until we can talk to our union.

SCENE 76. INT. KELTY'S OFFICE – ACTU. DAY.

Combet's head appears in the door of Kelty's office. He's pale, focussed, already running on adrenalin.

COMBET: Lockout at Webb Dock.

Kelty is on his feet and moving.

KELTY: Okay. Go. It's yours, Greg. (*Patting Combet on the chest*) And don't –

COMBET: – Fuck it up.

SCENE 77. INT./EXT. COMBET'S CAR – MELBOURNE DOCK. DAY.

Combet driving from the city down to the Melbourne docklands. Hyped, nervous, wondering what's in store.

NEWSREADER: (*on the radio*) … The chairman of Patrick Corporation, Chris Corrigan, has announced that he has agreed to lease surplus capacity and equipment at Melbourne's Webb Dock to the National Farmer's Federation …

CORRIGAN: (*on the radio*) After two years of fruitless negotiations we've decided to take action. It's our only chance to stem losses of what are now millions of dollars …

NEWSREADER: (*on the radio*) The NFF are establishing a new stevedoring operation, staffed by non-union labour, to be known as Producers and Consumers Stevedores …

Combet turns a corner and the security gate to Webb Dock's Patrick terminal comes into view. He can make out an untidy, confused and aggressive cluster of wharfies hanging on the cyclone wire beside the gate.

SCENE 78. INT. AN ABC TELEVISION STUDIO. DAY.

John Coombs faces the interviewer.

INTERVIEWER: So you're suggesting this move by the NFF is a provocation? To push the union into falling foul of the new legislation?

COOMBS: It's not legitimate. It's just another part of Reith's diabolical plan to create mayhem on the Australian waterfront.

SCENE 79. EXT. MAIN GATE – WEBB DOCK. DAY.

Screams of 'Scab' and a variety of obscenities are being hurled through the open gates at the security guards.

In truth, the wharfies are just a bit intimidated by the sheer unmoving bulk of the guards. These blokes aren't even raising a sweat.

A rugged, broken-nosed bloke with scars, tats and a seriously bad beer gut shapes up to the guards. Podge.

PODGE: Okay. Come on, youse scab mongrels. I'll have yas.

The boys in blue don't blink.

I said I'll fuckin' have yas.

Podge rocks back and forth, clearly preparing for a run at the gates. Combet, heading towards this confrontation, closes his eyes for a second, fearing a maiming or worse. But when he opens his eyes, Podge has only moved a couple of feet, and is feinting this way and that like an ageing heavyweight boxer.

I'll fuckin' have yas, all right.

And Combet involuntarily starts to smile, then grin, then laugh. He puts his head down, hand over his mouth to hide his level of amusement at Podge's expense. He calls out.

COMBET: Podge …

And Podge is instantly a pussycat. Mightily relieved at the interruption.

PODGE: Oh, g'day, Mr Combet. Just giving these scabs a bit of their own medicine. Hope it didn't offend you or nothing …

COMBET: Not at all. Keep up the good work. The other blokes still inside?

PODGE: Need a real silver tongue to get 'em out now. Someone snuck in a couple of slabs.

Combet takes this in, nods, pats Podge on the shoulder …

COMBET: As you were.

… And, already rehearsing his spin, he walks up to the biggest and meanest looking man in blue, speaks quietly to him, and slips inside the gate.

SCENE 80. INT. THE AMENITIES ROOM – PATRICK'S MELBOURNE DOCK. DAY.

Brendan turns into the room from where he leans down into the stairwell.

BRENDAN: It's Combet.

CHOPPER: Who?

NUTS: What?

BRENDAN: Greg Combet, you bogan. ACTU. Heard o' them? Affiliation of trade unions formed to devise policy and lobby on behalf of the labour movement.

Combet moves in behind Brendan.

COMBET: G'day fellas …

Replies from the wharfies. 'Greg' 'G'day, mate' 'Wanna beer?'

No, no. No thanks, mate.

His eyes scan the room. There's about thirty blokes in there. A number of them have been drinking. His brain ticks over rapidly, working out how to handle this. And what he's thinking is: 'Leadership credentials being put to the test. Big time. Don't fuck it up'.

Well, ah … the reason I've called you all here …

A couple of titters.

Okay. Look. Things are happening very fast here, but if we let it boil over, I think we're rooted. We've got to be a bit smart and a bit strategic about this …

TONY: Sorry, mate. We're not leavin' this room 'til they get that mob of fuckin' scabs out of here. Corrigan locks us outside that gate and we're going to need Semtex to get back in.

COMBET: What are you going to achieve by staying here? And for how long? 'Cos sooner or later you're going to get pretty hungry. And very on the nose.

CHOPPER: It's okay, mate. Legs's gone out for pizzas.

'Great', thinks Combet.

COMBET: Come on, fellas. You lot know the drill. Most of you've been in more stoppages than I've had hot dinners. We need to get some kind of discipline happening. I'm here representing Bill Kelty, okay? The MUA has a strategy and the ACTU is behind you all the way. Whatever's going on we'll get to the bottom of it and we'll take it on. But you blokes've got to work with us. And that means coming out of here, coming outside the gates, and staying calm.

TONY: Listen, I know you mean well, Greg. But that's not the way we do things in the MUA.

Combet leans in and speaks quietly to Tony. Calm but lethal.

COMBET: I worked for the MUA. I learned everything I know at the feet of Tas Bull. There's not a fucking thing you can tell me about how the MUA does things that I don't know ten times over. Now shut the fuck up and help me talk these blokes out of here before they're completely rat-arsed and we've got Armageddon on our hands.

SCENE 81. EXT. MAIN GATE – WEBB DOCK. EVENING.

A pyramid of discarded beer cans, maybe five, six feet high, surrounded by a cluster of now very drunk, very aggro wharfies. From the top of the pile protrudes a rough sign that reads: 'Club Webb'.

Sean, just looking at this. Oh, shit.

SEAN: Guys. Some of you know me. Some don't. I'm Sean McSwain, state rep for the union. We need to get off the piss, calm down, and get motivated here.

And with that a beer can whizzes through the air and just clips Sean on the side of the head. And two wharfies are on him, pulling him down into a brawl on the ground.

SCENE 82. EXT. MAIN GATE – WEBB DOCK. EVENING.

It is beginning to rain. The men from the amenities block are trudging out past the blue-clad security men. It's grudging, and Tony Tully shoots a final look to Combet as he goes. Combet is pacing, still inside the gate, talking on his mobile.

COMBET: Bill? Yeah, it's ugly. They're out of the amenities block, but it's ugly.

KELTY: (*on the phone*) You wanta set up a conference call with Coombs? He'll probably want to call them all out. Maybe P and O as well.

COMBET: I don't want anyone out, Bill. We'll talk about it when I get back, but I'll be advising John to keep them all working.

KELTY: (*on the phone*) *Are you on drugs?*

Combet quivers inside. Hold firm …

COMBET: You said I'd make the call.

A long, long silence.

KELTY: (*on the phone*) Okay. Do it your way.

And the phone is put down in Combet's ear.

It takes some moments for Combet to pull himself together, to breathe deeply, pull in the slight 'tall boy' hunch of his shoulders, raise himself up to his full height.

COMBET: (*voice over*) You might think us office types don't know how it feels. Natty ties, polished shoes. Ironed shirts.

SCENE 83. EXT. MAIN GATE – WEBB DOCK. EVENING.

It is now raining in earnest. Combet, rain dripping off his head and drenching his clothes, is addressing a crowd that is now several hundred strong. (Only some of this crowd are the locked-out workers – others are off-duty wharfies from other docks, friends, family, members of other trade unions.)

COMBET: You want to chuck Molotov cocktails over the fence.

You want to create mayhem so they all know how it feels. But I'm going to ask you to do something much harder than that. If we use violence, if we get pissed and pull on a barney, much as we might want to, then we're playing right into the hands of these bastards. They can say to the world – in front of all these cameras here – 'See, we were right, the wharfies really are a bunch of thugs'. Let's not give them that chance. In twenty minutes a van's going to be coming through. It's going to be full of security guards. I'm going to ask you to do the hardest thing. Do not touch that van. You can yell, you can say whatever you like. But do not resort to physical violence. The whole country's watching you. Show them you've got discipline. And that you know every other unionist, all over the country, tens of thousands of them, are on your side. And that you know, whatever it takes, you will be back inside that gate.

Sean is hanging back in the shadows, among the men, watching this. Admiring.

Combet, aware of a presence beside him, looks up. To find Podge holding an umbrella over his head.

SCENE 84. EXT. MAIN GATE – WEBB DOCK. NIGHT.

A white security van has pulled up a couple of hundred yards from the gates. Now it starts to move. Very slowly.

Combet watches. Sean. Brendan and Tony Tully. The van gets closer. Closer. It is not going to stop. The wharfies move in to surround it. Combet holds his breath. The world goes into slow motion and the sound is muted. The wharfies scream abuse at the van, shake their fists at it, yell obscenities. Combet watches them – looking at one face after the other – seeing the fear and anger and humiliation. But not one *of them touches the van.*

The van moves through and inside the gate. And the gate is padlocked shut.

For the second time on this awful night Combet breathes with relief and feels his mobile phone ringing in his pocket. He answers it, moving away from the crowd so he can hear.

COMBET: John. It's good to hear your voice, mate.

His own voice is starting to crack, growing hoarse. He's drenched. And he's getting the flu.

SCENE 85. INT. COOMBS' OFFICE – MUA. NIGHT.

Coombs is pacing his office. Intercut with:

SCENE 86. EXT. MAIN GATE – WEBB DOCK. NIGHT.

Outside, his staff are clustered around. No one can possibly leave on this night. Coombs, stuck in Sydney, desperately wants to be down there with his men. He is distressed, agitated.

Combet is walking in the darkness of the docks. In contrast to Coombs he is almost unreasonably calm.

COOMBS: ... Can't just do nothing. They'll tear the joint apart. We've got to picket. We've got to call a stoppage. We've got to let them see we're fighting for them.

COMBET: That's exactly what they want. Reith. Howard. Can't you see? They're trying to provoke us into action so they can pull the Trade Practices Act down on our heads. They're playing us like mugs. And we'll be mugs if we fall into it.

COOMBS: Who runs this union?

COMBET: You do.

COOMBS: But you're the big-picture man, aren't you, Greg?

COMBET: Why do I think that's not a compliment?

Silence. Combet's voice is close to a whisper now, cracking.

You think I'm this rational fuckin' dickhead, don't you? All head, no heart. You always have. I'm ... here, John. I'm looking at the fear in their faces. You think I've worked this hard to sell these men down the river? Maybe I've got no right to. I've never worked beside them, or been godfather to their kids. I can't even drive a crane. But I'm not a machine, John. I love these blokes ...

Coombs hesitates, unsure.

Trust me, John. Please, mate.

An almost interminable silence, then:

COOMBS: Yeah. Righto. Go home and get some rest, will you? You sound like shit.

And the line is severed.

SCENE 87. INT. CORRIGAN'S OFFICE – PATRICK HEAD OFFICE. NIGHT.

Corrigan and a couple of his staff are watching the late ABC News live from Webb Dock.

Greg Combet is being interviewed. He is wet, pale, looking stunned under the lights.

COMBET: What I think we need to understand here is that this is not just about wharfies. It's about every single worker in this country ...

Corrigan studies Combet's face. Almost an echo of the earlier scene. As though he, too, is studying his nemesis.

SCENE 88. INT. THE LIVING ROOM – COOMBS' HOUSE. NIGHT.

John, Gwen and Garry Coombs, also watching the report.

COMBET: (*on television*) ... It's not just about the Maritime Union. It's about every union. It's not just about a few hundred jobs. It's about thousands and thousands of jobs all over the country. Because if this can happen to these workers, then no worker, anywhere in the country, is safe ...

COOMBS: 'Trust me', he says. Jesus Christ, I hope he's right. 'Cos if he's not I'm going to go down in history as the bloke who let the union be destroyed on his watch.

SCENE 89. EXT. MAIN GATE – WEBB DOCK. NIGHT.

Combet is walking away from the cameras and the lights, from the knots of wet and angry men, back towards his car. He encounters Sean, who is looking very much the worse for wear after his brawl with the men. He is taking a private few moments to try to clean his face up with a rain-wet hanky.

Sean manages a rather pained grin.

COMBET: Our blokes? Or theirs? Don't answer that.

SEAN: Want to hear something funny? I just got the nod today.

Both of them grin hugely at the irony. Sean is bleeding, Combet full of flu.

COMBET: Mate. Hearty congratulations.

SEAN: Thanks, mate. Just remind me why we do this gig? Something about the unions underpinning the labour movement –

COMBET: '... The foundation stone upon which we build a vision of social justice and a fair go for all.' What fuckin' nob thought that sounded like a good idea?

SEAN: Found a horse float to kip down in for the duration. Don't reckon I'm going to be seeing my kids for a while, am I?

Combet doesn't answer. His eyes scan the men standing in the rain. The security guards. The docks and the cranes in the distance.

COMBET: I remember when I first started, Tas used to say: 'No matter what they might try to tell you different, Greg, always remember: –'

SEAN *and* COMBET: '– We own the waterfront'.

COMBET: You've heard it?

SEAN: I read all his speeches.

COMBET: We won it fair and square back in the forties. The waterfront's ours, brother ... Don't think any of us are going to be seeing our kids for a while, mate.

And he begins to walk back towards his car, into the distance. Fade to black.

END OF PART ONE

SCENE 1. INT./EXT. SUBURBAN HOUSE AND BACKYARD. DAY.

A young man with a very short military haircut, wearing a slouch hat, a singlet and nothing else, carries a shotgun over his shoulder as he marches back and forth, back and forth across the yard, doing parade type turns at each end. His naked bottom wobbles as he marches.

SOLDIER: We're gunna fuck the wharfies ... We're gunna fuck the wharfies ... We're gunna fuck the wharfies ...

This childish sing-song chant continues, muted, as, drawing back, and back again, through the window of the house, an ageing woman is revealed furtively picking up a telephone and dialling.

SCENE 2. INT. LIMBO. DAY.

John Coombs addresses the camera.

COOMBS: Oh, mate, the you-know-what was flying in every direction. We had calls coming in from all over, rumours you can't even imagine about what the other side was up to ... One old dear called up with a story about her nephew in the back yard ... It'd turn your hair, I tell you. And all the rumours came down to the same thing: ... the whole lot was going to hit the fan at Easter ...

Super caption: 'John Coombs, Secretary, Maritime Union of Australia'.

SCENE 3. INT. LIMBO. DAY.

Greg Combet addresses the camera.

Josh's war: Josh Bornstein (Justin Smith) alone on the court steps.

COMBET: I guess you'd call it a kind of phoney war. They were trying to screw us, and we were trying to screw them. To put it politely.

Super caption: 'Greg Combet, Assistant Secretary, ACTU'.

SCENE 4. INT. LIMBO. DAY.

Josh Bornstein, 32, addresses the camera.

JOSH: Upset? I was bloody ropable. To put it bluntly, I thought the union were lying down and saying 'Fuck me'. In any position you like.

Super caption: 'Josh Bornstein, solicitor, Maurice, Blackburn, Cashman'.

BASTARD BOYS:
PART TWO: JOSH'S WAR

SCENE 5. EXT. MAIN GATE – WEBB DOCK. NIGHT.

A crowd of several hundred people clustered around the locked security gate.

Media cameras, reporters and microphones. Choppers hovering overhead. Perhaps even a view down from one of them.

Snatches of radio voice over:

COOMBS: (*voice over*) They have locked us out of the place. It's a union-busting scam. The Federal Government is behind it.

INTERVIEWER: (*voice over*) But, technically, you're not locked out, are you? It's only one berth at Webb Dock that Patrick has leased out ...

CORRIGAN: (*voice over*) This is not – I repeat – *not* a lockout. It suits the union to say that, but if they do not return to work on the other berths at Webb Dock we will be forced to take legal action.

SCENE 6. EXT. – ANNA'S SCHOOL AND STREET. DAY.

Greg Combet and Anna walk out of the school building. Greg glances at his watch. He's late and he's worried. He leans down to Anna.

ANNA: 'Bye, Dad.

COMBET: 'Bye, sweetheart. See you tonight.

He gives her a quick kiss goodbye and she goes back inside. Combet turns and moves at speed out the gate and towards his car, already speed-dialling on his mobile phone.

SCENE 7. INT. RECEPTION – ACTU. DAY.

Greg Combet hurries into the ACTU reception area.

COMBET: Sorry sorry sorry. Parent-teacher.

The receptionist is listening hard to a call. He waves his hand, indicating Combet's office, and hands him a card: 'Josh Bornstein. Maurice, Blackburn, Cashman Solicitors'.

SCENE 8. INT. COMBET'S OFFICE – ACTU. DAY.

Combet enters to find Josh looking at the array of union campaign posters around the walls.

COMBET: Josh Bornstein.

JOSH: Greg Combet.

They shake hands. Combet waits.

This Patrick thing. I want to discuss your legal strategy.

COMBET: Well, our industrial strategy's to –

JOSH: No. Your *legal* strategy.

COMBET: Ah, well, we haven't really got one yet.

JOSH: You haven't *got* one?

COMBET: Truth is, we're flying by the seat of our pants.

SCENE 9. EXT. WEBB DOCK. DAY.

Sean McSwain is sitting in a horse float, trying – rather hazardously – to shave with a cup of water and a blunt razor, as a police sergeant talks to him.

SERGEANT 1: The buses with the PCS men …

SEAN: Scabs.

SERGEANT 1: Whatever. They'll be coming through in about half an hour.

SEAN: I want to talk to the drivers first. Shit …

Another shaving cut.

SERGEANT 1: I want a guarantee of no violence.

SEAN: What am I, mate? Gandhi?

The cop grins and pats the top of his head.

SERGEANT 1: Hope not. If you had to do the top as well, you'd damn near bleed to death.

They look up as a ferociously noisy, hotted up, resprayed old Holden or Valiant does a spectacular wheelie behind the group at the docks. Heads turn. From this beast climb Tony and Brendan Tully. The cavalry has arrived.

TONY: At ease, boys. The Tully gang's here.

Brendan is pulling something from the boot of his car.

SEAN: Where've you been?

TONY: Night shift over at East Swanston. Day shift here. Watch this.

Brendan is now shaping up like an athlete, warming up, crouching, stretching, then leaning forward into a sprinter's position. And, as though an imaginary gun has fired, he sprints at full force towards the fence. He's Rambo, Arnie, Van Damme. And with one mighty leap he jumps almost to the top of the fence, steadies, and then raises what looks like a kind of sling shot affair. He spins it in the air … whoosh … whoosh … whoosh … then releases it. The 'something' turns out to be a giant flour bomb, and it lands close enough to a small cluster of security guards to cover them head to foot in a mixture of flour and what might be either mud or cow dung.

BRENDAN: *Scabs!*

An outbreak of applause from the gathered picketers. Brendan, atop the fence, smiles and bows in appreciation.

TONY: Just like the old days …

Brendan's eyes fall on the cop, who is gesturing to him ominously. Come here, son …

SCENE 10. INT. COMBET'S OFFICE – ACTU. DAY.

Greg and Josh.

JOSH: What do unions traditionally do at times like this?

COMBET: Take industrial action. But –

JOSH: You're not doing that. Why?

COMBET: You know why. Under the new legislation they'd fine us to hell and back.

JOSH: What unions do at times like this: they react. The enemy acts. The unions react. The march is stolen on them. And it's goodnight, nurse.

Combet thought he was a young Turk. This uppity young lawyer is even younger.

COMBET: Yeh, righto. I assume you haven't come in here just to tell me how to do my job. So what've you got?

JOSH: Get on the front foot. Attack first.

COMBET: What with? A bazooka?

JOSH: A conspiracy case.

COMBET: Go on.

JOSH: Bring an action in the Federal Court against Patrick, the National Farmers' Federation, and, if I'm right and they're behind it, the government. For conspiring to diminish the terms and conditions of your guys for no other reason than that they are members of a union. Section 298K. The right to freedom of association. Howard's breaking his own law.

Combet is blown away. Suddenly a whole new world of possibility is opening to him. His brain starts rapidly ticking over.

COMBET: ... Take the Federal Government to court for conspiracy?

Josh is unstoppable. He's like a mini whirlwind.

JOSH: It's never been done before, but we can do it. It's fuckin' visionary. We can make a statement that says government and big business can shake each other's dicks all they like, but they won't get away with it. That you cannot legally arsehole a legitimate workforce. That aspiring for more and more obscene profit margins to satisfy –

COMBET: We?

JOSH: I'm a Jewish kid from socialist parents who went to Melbourne Grammar. I've got all bases covered. I know how the power elite works. I know who's in bed with whose wife. And I know this government wants to shaft you guys so hard you'll never walk again. There are legal teams assembling all over town as we speak, waiting to lay you in the dirt and pick the flesh off your carcass. If we can pull this thing off it'll be the most monumentally important thing we'll ever do in our lives.

Combet looks at him, assessing. Is he offering a real solution? Can he be trusted?

Pro bono. Take it or leave it.

COMBET: Pardon?

JOSH: Pro bono. It means for nothing. I'll do it for nothing.

COMBET: I know what it means.

Josh's excitement is starting to infect him.

But – just for the record – I do the Marxist raves around here. Okay?

SCENE 11. INT. RECEPTION – ACTU. DAY.

John Coombs, carrying an overnight bag, walks into the reception area.

COOMBS: All right. Where's this hotshot whiz kid who's going to save our bacon?

SCENE 12. INT. THE BOARDROOM – ACTU. DAY.

Kelty, Combet, Coombs and ACTU president Jennie George are assembled to listen to Josh present his proposed strategy. Rapid, overlapping dialogue.

KELTY: Get the men to do *what*?

JOSH: Go back to work. On every berth at Webb Dock except Number Five. You'll have to sooner or later –

COOMBS: Work on one end of a dock with scabs up the other while a bunch of wankers ponce around in wigs and gowns. It won't be pretty.

KELTY: Why the blazes don't we just shut Corrigan down? He hasn't got anyone trained. We pull out of every Patrick dock in the country and he's stuffed –

COMBET: Ah … John and I have been discussing this –

COOMBS: (*interrupting*) If I call a national stoppage I've blown the only shot I've got. We pull it on now, we've got twenty-four hours of chaos, and then what? We've got nothing left.

JOSH: John's right. You've got to use brains, not brawn. Co-ordinate your industrial strategy with your PR strategy and sue them before they sue you.

KELTY: (*to Combet*) This bloke ever met a wharfie?

Coombs puts up a hand to calm Kelty.

COOMBS: Wait on … (*To Combet*) This is where the conspiracy thing comes in, is it … ?

COMBET: Precisely. I've been trying to find an angle on this thing for weeks, Bill. I think this might be it.

SCENE 13. EXT. BANKSTOWN CAR PARK. DAY.

January 31st, 1998. A blisteringly hot day. A motorcycle turns into a half empty, drab and unkempt car park in western Sydney. A figure climbs off and removes his helmet. Chris Corrigan.

He looks around. Where the fuck am I?

And spies a single car, some distance away. One window slides down and Peter Kilfoyle lifts a hand in acknowledgement.

SCENE 14. INT./EXT. CAR – BANKSTOWN CAR PARK. DAY.

Corrigan climbs into the car and faces Mike Wells and Peter Kilfoyle.

KILFOYLE: Chris.

CORRIGAN: Mike. Peter. How are you?

KILFOYLE: We're fine, mate. Problem is, our blokes aren't fine. 'Cos we promised them a job. And now you've got the farmers in at Webb our blokes are like seventy-six proverbial spare pricks.

CORRIGAN: That's a lot of pricks.

SCENE 15. INT. BAR NEAR MELBOURNE COURTS. EVENING.

A doorstop interview with Chris Corrigan is on a television screen in the corner of a small, quiet bar. It is watched intensely by Josh Bornstein and Greg Combet as they have a beer together.

SYDNEY JOURNALIST: (*on television*) What is the link between the Webb Dock enterprise and the Dubai scheme, and what is your role?

CORRIGAN: (*on television*) There is no link. Dubai is history. I have no role in it.

Combet is drawing more and more complex diagrams on a series of coasters.

COMBET: One: someone – we don't know who – tries to train wharfies in Dubai. Two: the farmers' federation sets up a stevedoring company. Are they linked to Dubai? We don't know. Three: Corrigan leases them one berth at Webb. Why's he leasing his docks to competitors? None of it hangs together into any kind of pattern ...

JOSH: We've got to find the connections. And make 'em stand up in court. We're going to need a silk.

COMBET: We usually use Richard ...

JOSH: Nuh. We need a silk with right-wing respectability.

COMBET: I'd rather have one with the right politics.

JOSH: Bullshit. You need a rock star, from their own camp. Scare the living crap out of them. Politics is irrelevant. It's the purity of the law that matters.

Combet nearly sprays beer everywhere.

COMBET: The law? The *law*? With all respect, the law is an artificial construct erected by the capitalist class to ensure the system protects their own interests and maximises their own profit.

The two of them eye each other for a moment.

JOSH: Do you need proof of my credentials before you'll get into bed with me, Greg?

A shrug from Combet.

My father was a state Labor MP. My mother was an organiser for the Missos Union. My stepfather's been on the Industrial Relations commission. My great great uncle was Harry Bridges. There's my ALP membership card.

Game set and match to Josh.

COMBET: I thought my cred was pretty good.

JOSH: Ah, but you can take the boy out of Sydney ... What'd your old man do?

Combet looks down, stifles a grin, pauses for a long time.

COMBET: My old man ... made champagne.

Now it's Josh's turn to splutter his beer. And for a moment the two of them are laughing. A partnership is born.

SCENE 16. EXT. CORRIGAN'S HOUSE. EVENING.

Sydney. Corrigan's motorcycle turns off the street, comes down the driveway and drives into the underground car park.

SCENE 17. INT. THE HALLWAY – CORRIGAN'S HOUSE. EVENING.

An attractive woman in her late forties is sorting a large pile of mail. One letter in particular draws her attention. She opens it, and the words 'DIE SCABS' jump out at her.

Corrigan comes up the stairs from the car park, helmet in hand.

Valerie rapidly pushes the letter into her pocket and puts on her best smile. She moves to Corrigan and they embrace.

VALERIE: Claude's here. He's casing the joint.
CORRIGAN: Where are the kids?
VALERIE: Upstairs. Joe got selected for the choir.
CORRIGAN: Good on him.

SCENE 18. INT. THE LIVING ROOM – CORRIGAN'S HOUSE. EVENING.

They move through to where Claude, the chief of their chosen security operation, is assessing the living area.

CORRIGAN: How are you, Claude? Sorry I'm late.
CLAUDE: All this glass is a problem.
CORRIGAN: Sorry?
CLAUDE: I've been telling Mrs Corrigan about the division of labour. (*To Valerie*) Keep the kids at home as much as possible – invite their friends here rather than them going out. Do your shopping in different places – we'll send a bloke with you. Otherwise, try to run things as normally as possible. We've all got jobs to do here. (*Gesturing to Corrigan*) His is to fix the docks. Yours is to keep him healthy, focussed and on top of it. And ours is to keep you all safe.
VALERIE: What about school holidays?
CLAUDE: You mean Easter. Isn't that when … ?
CORRIGAN: I want you and the kids as far away from here as possible.
CLAUDE: I second that a hundred per cent.

Valerie looks like she's about to protest.

CORRIGAN: There you are. You've been told.

VALERIE: You set that up, didn't you?

Corrigan just looks at her over the top of his glasses. And smiles.

SCENE 19. INT. ENTRANCE HALL AND SITTING ROOM – JOSH'S MOTHER'S HOME. NIGHT.

A Melbourne upper-middle-class home, somewhere in Kew or Hawthorn. A slightly nervous Josh Bornstein is taking his new girlfriend, Tali, to dinner at the home of his mother and stepfather, who stand in the doorway to welcome them.

SIMON: Josh. And you must be Tali.

JOSH: Tali, Simon, my stepfather. And my mum. Judith.

TALI: Hi, Judith. Pleased to meet you.

JUDITH: (*with meaning*) So are we.

Josh gives her a glare: it's nerve-wracking to put the new girlfriend on display for the family.

He trails them into the sitting room where glasses of wine are poured and they sit down with olives and nibbles. These are educated, relatively affluent people, but the atmosphere should be informal and relaxed.

SIMON: Little bird tells me you've offered yourself to the union over this Webb Dock thing. What are you going on? Freedom of association?

JOSH: Conspiracy.

SIMON: (*impressed*) Whoooh. Okay. It's crazy …

JOSH *and* SIMON: … But it just might work.

There's real affection between Josh and Simon. Simon is his mentor.

JOSH: I'm on a bit of a promise not to talk about it too much tonight. I've been going on and on like some kind of crazed zealot.

TALI: He has, actually.

JUDITH: Oh, well, we'll just have to content ourselves with Josh's other peccadillos. Has he told you about the gee-gees?

JOSH: I like horse racing. The family think it's a form of genetic weakness.

TALI: You like horse racing.

JOSH: So … all bets are off?

TALI: The odds are shortening … lengthening … whatever odds do …

JOSH: Come on. Melbourne cup. Race day at Randwick.

JUDITH: Ah. Randwick. That's another problem.

SIMON: Judith. Leave the poor boy alone …

Tali is looking bewildered, Josh embarrassed.

JUDITH: You see, Randwick's in Sydney.

TALI: And?

JUDITH: Josh is scared of flying.

Josh rolls his eyes to heaven.

JOSH: Kill me now.

SCENE 20. INT./EXT. JOSH'S CAR – TALI'S STREET. NIGHT.

Josh and Tali are parked outside her place.

JOSH: Thanks for tonight. Simon's … well, his opinion means a lot to me.

TALI: His opinion of me?

Josh smiles, nods. Yeah, you got me.

JOSH: They liked you. I'm sorry we talked about the case so much. It'll sound conceited. But I think I was born to fight this case. *Does* it sound conceited?

TALI: Yes.

JOSH: Um. Look, I'm pretty high-maintenance. Tali. Unfortunately, I seem to have this fatal attraction for high-maintenance women. Irresistible force meets immovable object kind of thing.

TALI: 'Artistic' types?

JOSH: Just let me get this out before you take the piss, will you? I just – I'm sorry if this sounds hard – I don't want to go there with you if it's going to be the same thing.

TALI: Oh, I'm not at all artistic.

A shared grin.

So, do I tell them at Slater and Gordon that I'm sleeping with the enemy, or what?

JOSH: Maybe you can tell them you've met the enemy's mother.

TALI: Dead giveaway.

They're both laughing. And the next thing they know they're kissing.

SCENE 21. INT. RECEPTION – ABC TV STUDIO. NIGHT.

Sydney. Chris Corrigan and Paul walk through the reception area.

PAUL: Chris. This interview's going to be pretty delicate stuff ...

CORRIGAN: If you're telling me not to fuck it up, I'm onto it.

With which he walks straight into a pole.

PAUL: Chris. Pole.

Corrigan shrugs sheepishly.

SCENE 22. INT. ABC TV STUDIO. NIGHT.

February 3rd, 1998. An ABC journalist, ideally Tony Jones on Lateline*, addresses the camera.*

ABC JOURNALIST: The boss of Patrick Stevedores, Chris Corrigan, has today made a surprise public admission.

Corrigan faces the music.

Chris Corrigan. You've consistently said you had no role at all in the Dubai training operation. Why did you lie?

CORRIGAN: What I'm telling you is that I had a *limited role only* in the Dubai matter. Leasing premises, equipment. That's all.

ABC JOURNALIST: And so why did you lie?

CORRIGAN: I was afraid the union would shut me down.

ABC JOURNALIST: And this consortium. Was it Fynwest? Was it Peter Kilfoyle? Did you have a direct relationship with them?

CORRIGAN: No.

SCENE 23. INT. COMBET'S OFFICE – ACTU. DAY.

Melbourne. Once again, this interview is being watched by Josh, Coombs and Combet on the television in Combet's office. As usual, Combet watches Corrigan with intensity.

Combet picks up a photograph of Peter Kilfoyle, which sits on his desk. He picks up the phone receiver on the landline and holds it to Coombs.

Coombs pulls a coin from his pocket.

COOMBS: Call.

COMBET: Tails.

Tails it is. Combet's 'it'.

Dunno why I bother ...

He begins to dial.

JOSH: Uh-uh. Digital to digital, remember. Comrade.

He tosses Combet's mobile over. Combet grins. Fair call. And dials.

COMBET: Peter Kilfoyle? Greg Combet from the ACTU. I got a message you wanted to talk to us.

Josh starts to grin.

JOSH: This is so John Le Carré.

SCENE 24. INT. THE ESPLANADE HOTEL – ST KILDA. DAY.

February 4th, 1998. Coombs and Combet, both in suits and ties, stand in the hotel. Coombs is nervously shifting his weight from one foot to the other.

COOMBS: All right. What now?

COMBET: We're early. Just relax.

Coombs looks at him. And just how relaxed are you?

Yeah. Right.

COOMBS: Come on. At least we can get a bloody beer out of this peanut hunt.

They move in the direction of the bar. And suddenly both realise, simultaneously, that, in suits and ties in this joint, they stand out like dog's balls.

What nob thought suits were a good idea?

He walks off towards the bar.

Combet sits down, trying desperately to look both calm and inconspicuous. Failing dismally.

Two beers are plonked on the table.

COMBET: Would've preferred water, John.

COOMBS: Jesus Christ. You're in a flaming bloodhouse looking like something out of a Fletcher Jones catalogue. Just how much more of a prize twat d'you wanta be, Greg?

And now they see the following: a tall, bulky man in a large vest approaches down the grand staircase at the back of the hotel. He glances around furtively, then strides across the pub and stands a metre away from them.

KILFOYLE: Sorry I'm late. Just checking the exit strategy. Peter Kilfoyle.

COMBET: Ah, Greg Combet and ...

KILFOYLE: We know who you are.

He grips their hands, one after another, practically crushing them. Combet has his work cut out not to wince.

Then Kilfoyle turns and marches across the pub, the two unionists following. Combet looks at Coombs and mouths, '"Exit strategy"?'

SCENE 25. INT. THE ESPLANADE HOTEL – ST KILDA. DAY.

A waitress or barmaid is taking orders from Combet, Coombs, Kilfoyle and Kilfoyle's colleague McTernan.

KILFOYLE: I'll have three steak sandwiches with the lot.

COMBET: Just one, thanks.

Coombs and McTernan indicate they'd like a steak sandwich each.

KILFOYLE: (*to McTernan*) You check this joint out?

McTernan nods.

(*To Combet and Coombs*) Corrigan's a rat.

COMBET: I think we're across that one.

KILFOYLE: Oh, no, mate. You're not across anything. We enlist a mob of good blokes – decent blokes – to train 'em in Dubai. He's paying for every red cent of it. The shit hits the fan in the media. And now our fellas are left high and dry, all dressed up nowhere to go.

COOMBS: The same decent blokes who were going to take our jobs, you mean?

KILFOYLE: Not the fuckin' point.

He brings his open palm down hard on the table.

COMBET: Corrigan paid for it?

KILFOYLE: He's going to do you guys. He's got wall-to-wall security on all the docks – cameras, top-of-the-range surveillance stuff, hundreds of grand's worth.

COMBET: How do you know?

KILFOYLE: Mate, I installed it. This stuff's so good you can see the blackheads in a wharfie's ear.

He lets them absorb this.

He's going to lock youse out of Port Botany. He's got the troublemakers tabbed and followed. He's going to skin youse.

Coombs and Combet glance at each other.

COMBET: Why are you telling us this?

KILFOYLE: Insurance. We take out a lot of insurance. We've got tapes, we've got documents, we've got fingerprints. We could bust Corrigan apart. We could bust the Government apart.

Kilfoyle bangs his hand down on the table. Coombs and Combet try to control the impulse to jump.

Still think you're across it?

COMBET: Well, it would be nice to get all that.

KILFOYLE: Paul here's going to look after that. He's my business manager. And, in case you've got any ideas, we're taking out insurance with you guys too.

McTERNAN: There's a car round the corner. We're wearing directional microphones. Anything you say or do, we've got youse.

Coombs and Combet are too off balance to even look at each other now.

I'll give you the lot. But we want five point six for it.

COMBET: Five point six?

MCTERNAN: Mill. Compo for our blokes. And any trouble, we know where youse live.

He lifts a hand and aims a pretend gun at Combet's head.

The waitress plonks down the plates containing the steak sandwiches. Coombs and Combet look down at the lumps of meat on their plates, suddenly not hungry.

SCENE 26. INT./EXT. COMBET'S CAR – ST KILDA. DAY.

Coombs and Combet sitting in Combet's car. Stunned into near paralysis. Neither speaks. And then, ever so slowly, Combet starts to smile, then grin, then snigger, and then to just fall about laughing. After a moment, Coombs joins him.

COMBET: You know what we've been doing wrong all these years, John? We forgot to plan our exit strategy.

And they are pissing themselves with laughter. Clutching their stomachs. Combet banging his head again and again on the steering wheel.

From a distance, it looks like the car itself is shaking with laughter.

Above: Greg Combet (Daniel Fredriksen), John Coombs (Colin Friels), Paul McTernan (Keir Saltmarsh) and Peter Kilfoyle (Michael Robinson) negotiate. Below: Chris Corrigan (Geoff Morrell) asks a favour.

SCENE 27. INT. THE MEETING ROOM – MAURICE, BLACKBURN, CASHMAN. DAY.

Josh is tapping a pink-ribboned legal document. He's cool – he has a plan.

JOSH: As I predicted: Standard one twenty-seven action to force the men back to work at Webb. Which Corrigan'll win.

COOMBS: Yep.

COMBET: Can we spin it out to keep Webb down for as long as we can?

JOSH: Oh, I think so. And it might take even longer if we were to, say, subpoena the man himself. Get him on the stand as our witness.

Combet's instantly onto it. He starts to grin. Then nod.

COOMBS: Why in blazes would we want to do that?

COMBET: Because we can nail him – under oath. Flush him out about Dubai. Show the public what he's up to.

COOMBS: We know what he's flaming up to. Smashing the union with a bunch of cowboys who wouldn't know a portainer crane from a Matchbox toy.

COMBET: John, it's a PR exercise. He's been attacking our credibility for years. If we're gunna stand a snowball's chance in all this, we need the public on side. We need to make him look like the germ he is. Message management, mate.

COOMBS: Message management be buggered. He'll still win the case. And I'll still have a mutiny on my hands trying to get the blokes to work beside scabs.

COMBET: He'll win the case. But we'll win the public relations. There's more than one way of skinning the cat, brother. (*To Josh*) Thanks, Josh. Might be time you put the meter on, mate.

Josh, feet up on the table, cool as a cuke. Combet's not one to throw compliments around willy-nilly. And Josh is not going to show just how pleased he is by Combet's reaction.

SCENE 28. INT. CORRIGAN'S HOUSE. NIGHT.

Corrigan dials a number on his mobile phone.

WELLS: (*on the phone, muffled*) Chris Corrigan himself. How are you, Chris?

CORRIGAN: Mike, I need a favour. I need to get some documents back from you.

WELLS: (*on the phone, muffled*) You've still got one or two outstanding invoices from us, haven't you?

SCENE 29. EXT. MAIN GATE – WEBB DOCK. DAY.

A few moments of news footage of the protest at Webb Dock, then cut to …

SCENE 30. EXT. INDUSTRIAL RELATIONS COMMISSION. DAY.

… The IRC. A journalist addresses a news camera.

FEMALE ABC JOURNALIST: I'm here at the Federal Industrial Relations Commission where Patrick Stevedores is seeking an injunction to force the men back to work. Webb Dock has now been out of action for almost two weeks, inflicting considerable financial damage on Patrick, and, in a piece of carefully orchestrated theatre, Chris Corrigan, Patrick's CEO, is appearing as a witness, not for his own side, but actually subpoenaed by the union.

During this Chris Corrigan and his legal team attempt to make their way into the Commission room. They are surrounded by a media scrum – lights, cameras, microphones. At the centre of it all Corrigan looks like a startled rabbit in the headlights. His usual ease and confidence is nowhere to be seen.

SCENE 31. INT. INDUSTRIAL RELATIONS COMMISSION. DAY.

It is after 7 p.m. Outside the rain has cleared to become a stinking hot summer day. The room is packed and the air conditioning has broken down. Everyone is tired, tense and shining with sweat. Corrigan's legal team faces the union's legal team: Josh Bornstein, Greg Combet and other solicitors. John Coombs watches.

The whirring of press cameras is almost constant as Chris Corrigan takes the witness stand facing Greg Combet. It is a clash of two intimidatingly sharp intellects. And Combet is on a mission.

COMBET: Mr Corrigan. You gave evidence that you dealt with Mr Wells and Mr Kilfoyle earlier on: that is correct?

CORRIGAN: I had meetings with them, yes.

COMBET: Was that solely in relation to the sale of the straddle carriers?

PARRY: I object. He is leading the witness ...

COMMISSIONER: It's a bit late in the day for that, Mr Parry. He's been leading since he got on his feet.

CORRIGAN: Frankly, I'd be grateful if someone would lead me.

COMBET: And I think your evidence has been that not only did Patrick's involvement, as it were, in the Dubai operation go to the sale of the straddle carriers, but it went to some other aspects, did it not?

CORRIGAN: The commitment to lease Webb Dock.

COMBET: But can you give evidence that that was the full extent of Patrick's involvement in the Dubai operation?

CORRIGAN: Yes.

A look across the table between Combet and Josh. Josh scribbles something on a piece of paper, and hands it to Combet. Combet reads it, takes a breath, controls the desire to strangle Corrigan, and continues.

COMBET: How did you first come into contact with Mr Wells and Kilfoyle?

CORRIGAN: I think I was referred to them.

COMBET: Who referred you to Mr Wells and Mr Kilfoyle?

CORRIGAN: Well, nobody referred me to Mr Kilfoyle, but Mr Wells, I don't recall who referred me to him.

COMBET: That would appear somewhat unusual, would you agree, on such an important ...

PARRY: That is cross-examination. You asked a question and the answer has been given.

COMBET: So for what purpose did you approach Mr Wells, Mr Corrigan?

Corrigan pauses for some moments, choosing his words carefully.

CORRIGAN: I first approached him because I'd been asked to enquire about people who might be able to recruit and train suitable people, stevedoring people in Australia – sorry, not training in Australia, recruit in Australia, people for stevedoring.

Is Corrigan getting tired?

Combet is shimmering with contained anger. Hold it together, Greg. Josh watches him, alert. Hold it together ...

COMBET: So you approached Mr Wells in order to pursue an avenue for the recruitment of people to work in the stevedoring industry?

PARRY: Your Honour, it is cross-examination.

COMMISSIONER: Yes.

PARRY: It is again traversing the same issues.

COMBET: It is not traversing the same issues at all. Mr Corrigan, in his evidence so far, identified the extent of his commitment, as it were, to the Dubai operation as a commitment to lease Number Five Berth.

COMMISSIONER: Yes, I recall, yes.

COMBET: His evidence now is that that extends to the approaching of Mr Wells for the purpose of recruiting people to work in the stevedoring industry and I would submit that if that is not relevant to these proceedings, then I'm not too sure what is. I press the question.

PARRY: Well, I maintain the objection. It is leading.

COMMISSIONER: Answer the question, Mr Corrigan.

CORRIGAN: What was the question?

It's late. Everyone's tired, tense and frustrated, the only exception being Combet, who is fired by an explosive mixture of anger and adrenalin.

COMMISSIONER: This is the problem we always have.

COMBET: What was your objective in making this contact with Mr Wells, Mr Corrigan?

PARRY: He's already answered that question. He has given the answer to that. You can't keep asking a witness the same question.

SCENE 32. INT. AN ANTECHAMBER – INDUSTRIAL RELATIONS COMMISSION. NIGHT.

Josh, Coombs and Combet. Frustrated. Hot, tired and sweaty.

JOSH: You need to pin him down about his financial commitment.

COMBET: He's already said it. He said that was the full extent of Patrick's involvement.

JOSH: But there's more than one company. You've got to nail him across the board. Specific. Be specific.

SCENE 33. INT. INDUSTRIAL RELATIONS COMMISSION. NIGHT.

Combet takes a deep breath.

COMBET: Mr Corrigan, in taking the steps that you did to approach Mr Wells, what financial obligation if any, did that involve you or Patrick's in terms of the recruitment of personnel?

CORRIGAN: None.

The look between Josh and Combet.

COMBET: Well, Mr Corrigan, did Patrick Stevedoring accept any financial obligation at all in relation to the recruitment of the personnel?

CORRIGAN: No.

COMBET: Did Lang Corporation accept any financial obligation in terms of the recruitment of the personnel?

CORRIGAN: No.

COMBET: Did you yourself personally accept any financial obligation in relation to the recruitment of the personnel?

CORRIGAN: No.

Josh scribbles on a piece of paper and hands it to Combet.

Combet pauses for a long time.

COMBET: Have you discussed the notion of dismissing the workforce en masse with anyone outside your company?

Parry is instantly on his feet.

PARRY: My learned friend might have difficulty in asking a non-leading question …

COMBET: With respect, that was not a leading question. Have you had any discussion with anyone about the option of dismissing the workforce en masse?

COMMISSIONER: Yes, I will allow the question.

A long pause. Almost impossibly long.

CORRIGAN: I think the answer has to be 'Yes'.

A collective intake of breath all around the room. Coombs is tense. Several journalists begin to make their way out to file the story.

COMBET: Do you remember when any of those discussions took place?

CORRIGAN: I remember some discussions along those lines early in ninety-seven.

COMBET: And who were those discussions with?

CORRIGAN: I think they were with Government advisors.

Josh catches his breath – here it is. And this admission triggers an even larger exodus of reporters – they've got their story. The remainder of the scene takes place during this exodus.

COMBET: I've heard the name Webster mentioned … ?

CORRIGAN: No, not Webster. The one before Webster.

COMBET: Mr Bondo? Mr Gillespie?

CORRIGAN: No.
COMBET: A Mr Wallace?
CORRIGAN: Wallace, no.
COMBET: Mr Trebeck?
CORRIGAN: Trebeck, thank you. He obviously left a lasting impression.

SCENE 34. INT. AN ANTECHAMBER – INDUSTRIAL RELATIONS COMMISSION. NIGHT.

Combet, Coombs, Josh and a couple of other members of their legal team. Exhausted. Combet is close to completely rooted. His glasses are off, his head in his hands.

FEMALE ABC JOURNALIST: (*voice over*) This evening, after a long and very tense day, the Industrial Relations Commission ordered the MUA to return to work at Webb Dock. What was revealed, however, in an appearance by …

She fades out. Josh attempts to rally the troops.

JOSH: Hey, come on. We've done well. He's copped two weeks of industrial damage, and his reputation's down the tube.

Coombs is resigned to the outcome but, under the pressure of utter weariness, some of his feelings are on display …

COOMBS: Yeah, and my blokes have to work with a bunch of scabs. I know blokes down at Botany that've busted a gut for years on the docks. Generations of 'em. I know blokes dead at fifty from asbestos dust. Blokes crushed under containers, or smashed up on the steel ships … What were their lives worth? Nothing? All we've done. Stopping pig iron going to the Japs. Indonesia. Apartheid … And this is what we get?

He is practically crying.

JOSH: John, I want to go to the docks.
COOMBS: What on earth for?
JOSH: Just to look at the faces of the people I'm working for.
COOMBS: Don't be bloody stupid. You'd either get arrested or get yourself beaten up. Probably by our own blokes. Then where would I be? Sued for assault by my own flaming lawyer.

The following scenes might be slightly slowed or step printed. They are designed as mood pieces, accompanied by music, rather than actual dramatic scenes.

SCENE 35. INT. NEWS FOOTAGE. DAY.

Peter Reith, apparently in interview.

REITH: Quite frankly, I don't care if they arrive by boat, by jumbo, by helicopter, by jet pilot, by walking, by running or by bus …

SCENE 36. INT. THE LIVING ROOM – JOSH'S FLAT. NIGHT.

REITH: (*on television*) … The good news is that we have people who are today on the Melbourne docks, who are training for a new job and we're injecting some real competition into an industry that has been moribund for decades. Waterfront reform is, as every importer and exporter in the country knows, to his cost, long long overdue. To those Australians, this is nothing short of a dream come true …

Tali watches quietly while Josh, in a fit of anger, gropes around trying to find something, anything, to throw at the television screen. Finally he resorts to wrenching off his shoe and chucking that.

TALI: So – what – the scabs are still at Berth Five …

JOSH: … And our guys've got to go back to work on the other four berths … right fucking beside them …

TALI: Nice …

JOSH: Work a shift, man the picket. Same at East Swanston – that's the deal – work your shift, man the picket at Webb, work your shift … and that miserable prick has the gall to call them bludgers …

Above: Tali Bernard (Caroline Craig) and Josh Bornstein (Justin Smith) at home. Below: The Tullys, Tony (Jack Thompson) and Brendan (Daniel Wyllie) on the docks.

SCENE 37. EXT. MAIN GATE – WEBB DOCK. DAY.

Sean, surrounded by a number of men still protesting, watches as a line of men, faces set, pride badly damaged, file through the security gates to return to work. Tony and Brendan Tully are among them.

SCENE 38. INT./EXT. SECURITY BUS – MAIN GATE . DAY.

Sean leads the remaining protesters, shouting abuse, as the security bus drives the 'scabs' through the picket. Through the bus windows some faces can be seen: ordinary blokes who just want to work. Others have their heads down, or have jackets or balaclavas over their heads, afraid of union reprisals if they are recognised. Amongst them are two faces in particular: the soldier from the opening sequence. And Dan Brodie.

SCENE 39. INT./EXT. A CRANE – WEBB DOCK. DAY.

Dan Brodie, high up in a crane, is taking instruction from a trainer. He looks over the fence from Berth 5 to the other side of Webb Dock, where the union members are back at work. And there is a row of wharfies, naked bums in the air, giving him a collective 'brown eye'.

SCENE 40. INT. CITY ALLEYWAY. NIGHT.

Combet, Coombs and Josh wander into a badly lit Melbourne city alleyway.

Combet checks an address, then knocks on a door. Nothing. He knocks again. Still nothing. He pushes the door open and calls up a grimy stairwell.

COMBET: Hello? Hello?

SCENE 41. INT. THE STAIRWELL – THE KELVIN CLUB. NIGHT.

Combet leads the three into the stairwell.

COMBET: Hello?
COOMBS: Hello?

Still silence.

They move up the stairs ...

SCENE 42. INT. THE KELVIN CLUB. NIGHT.

... And find themselves in a dingy, badly lit, grimy bar which is completely empty. They look around. No one.

COMBET: Nice ambience ...

He shrugs, takes his jacket off, and sits at a table. Coombs and Josh follow. They sit in silence for what seems an eternity.

JOSH: Are we having a good time yet?

And now a very young waitress in a very short skirt appears.

WAITRESS: Hi. Can I get you boys a drink?

Josh almost snorts at the word 'boys'.

COOMBS: Three beers, thanks.
WAITRESS: VB, Carlton, Heineken, Corona, Coopers – ?
COOMBS: Carlton. Carlton. Whatever.

The girl goes off.

(*To Combet*) And not a fucking word about wanting water.

Another moment, and then, as though from nowhere, Peter Kilfoyle and Mike Wells emerge from behind a curtain.

General introductions and handshakes. 'Mike Wells'. 'Josh Bornstein, our lawyer.' Etcetera.

KILFOYLE: (*gesturing to Wells*) He's the brains of the operation.
COOMBS: Interesting place.
KILFOYLE: We have a lot of meetings here. No chance of being sprung in this place. We're all good boy scouts here.

He taps the breast of his jacket, indicating the presence of a weapon. Combet and Coombs study Mike Wells. A smallish man, older than Kilfoyle and without Kilfoyle's aggressive bluster, he almost has a kind of personal dignity. Up close, he looks rather unwell.

WELLS: We've got a lot in common, us and you blokes. I've established a reputation in this business – finding legitimate jobs for ex servicemen. We entered an agreement with Chris Corrigan in good faith, and we've been made to look dishonest and corrupt.

KILFOYLE: Our blokes have been called terrorists.

WELLS: Mercenaries.

KILFOYLE: Mercenaries. Yeah, that's right.

WELLS: And we're still having to push him to give them jobs with the farmers' mob.

KILFOYLE: (*gesturing to Wells*) He's been crook over it. Haven't you, matey?

Frankly, the unionists are uninterested in Wells' state of health. Nor the fate of a bunch of people they consider scabs.

COMBET: We're interested in having a look at the documents.

JOSH: Especially anything that implicates the government.

Wells opens a briefcase.

WELLS: They're copies. We had them certified by a registered accountant. See here: this is a true and certified copy of the original. Signed.

He lays a number of documents on the table. Josh begins to study them – although it's an uphill battle because the venue is so badly lit.

I've also got transcripts of meetings between me and Corrigan.

KILFOYLE: Told you we take insurance.

COMBET: Mr Bornstein's here to compare your version of events with Corrigan's evidence in court.

KILFOYLE: Huh. Corrigan wouldn't know the truth if it was up him in the hall of mirrors.

Josh continues looking through the documents as:

COOMBS: How much do you want for them?

WELLS: We're not in this for personal gain ...

KILFOYLE: That's right. Absolutely not. We just want compensation for our boys.

COOMBS: Several million of compensation, is that right?

During this, Josh leans in and murmurs to Combet.

JOSH: There's bank statements – payments from Patrick to Fynwest. Implicates him in bankrolling Dubai –

COMBET: Well, politically – (*'that's gold.'*)

JOSH: – But they're copies ... For all we know, they could be true and certified pieces of dunny paper. Legally, they're useless. They'd be laughed out of court.

COMBET: (*to Josh, sotto voce*) This is Mickey Mouse. These clowns are not going to save our bacon before Easter ...

SCENE 43. EXT. CITY ALLEYWAY. NIGHT.

The three pour out the door and back onto the street. And Josh promptly drops down in the middle of the laneway, lies on his back and moans up at the sky.

COOMBS: How, in the name of all that's holy, did Chris Corrigan get into bed with them?

COMBET: Maybe he didn't plan his exit strategy either.

Coombs and Combet start to walk off. Josh leans up on his elbow.

JOSH: Hey. I got us a silk. Julian Burnside.

COMBET: Burnside? But he's corporate. He's never even touched IR.

JOSH: Yep. A right-wing capitalist running dog. Never even opened the legislation. He's perfect.

COMBET: Oh, I get it. (*To a bewildered Coombs*) He's a rock star.

SCENE 44. EXT. THE FRONT GARDEN – BURNSIDE'S HOUSE. DAY.

Josh, Coombs and Combet standing in the sculpture-filled garden of a genteel Hawthorn house. They knock on the front door, which opens to reveal Julian Burnside. Anyone less like a rock star is difficult to imagine.

BURNSIDE: Come in, come in. Thanks so much for coming here. Much more comfortable than chambers ... Josh. Yes, yes, John Coombs. And Geoff. Good to meet you.

SCENE 45. INT. THE STUDY – BURNSIDE'S HOUSE. DAY.

Burnside's genteel study-library. A beautiful room lined with cabinets of books. Classical music plays quietly. Tea and cakes are on the table.

JOSH: ... Section two ninety-eight K is the guarantee of the right to freedom of association. Canberra stuck it in there to legislate away compulsory unionism. But, arguably, if you've got the right to not join a union, then you've also got the right to be a union member without being penalised for it.

BURNSIDE: This is the Workplace Relations Act we're talking about, is it? I've not read it.

He is rolling a roll-your-own cigarette.

Hope you don't mind if I smoke. It helps me concentrate. I feel much the same about Pepsi cola, actually. More coffee, Geoff?

Combet graciously allows the wrong name to pass.

COMBET: Thanks. There's absolutely no doubt that Peter Reith is making an example of this union ... if the MUA goes down, the CFMEU'll be next, then ...

BURNSIDE: You should know I'm not political, Geoff. To be honest, politics appals me.

An awful hiatus. Josh rushes to the rescue.

JOSH: Uh, John and *Greg* are anxious about the rumours that're circulating ... talking about a move on the docks at Easter ... 'Sonly a couple of weeks away ...

Move away from them now. It's not necessary to hear the detail.

SCENE 46. INT./EXT. THE BACK GARDEN – BURNSIDE'S HOUSE. DAY.

The group is visible through the window. Burnside just listens. He has a slight tic in one eye when he's concentrating, the machinery of his brain whirring.

SCENE 47. INT./EXT. A GOVERNMENT OFFICE. DAY.

Corrigan is visible through the window of a government office building talking to someone out of view.

CORRIGAN: We're talking about a hundred and fifty-eight million in redundancy payouts. I can't go any further without a firm commitment at your end.

His interlocutor is revealed: Peter Reith.

SCENE 48. EXT. THE FRONT YARD – COMBET'S HOUSE. NIGHT.

Combet walks in the front gate. He's tired. He walks round the side of the house.

SCENE 49. EXT. THE BACKYARD – COMBET'S HOUSE. NIGHT.

Combet fills up the feed and water containers for his birds. Unshakable discipline in the face of utter exhaustion.

SCENE 50. INT. THE HALLWAY AND ANNA'S ROOM – COMBET'S HOUSE. NIGHT.

The house is in darkness. Combet is making his way quietly down the hall towards the bedroom when he hears:

ANNA: (*out of view*) Dad?

Combet sticks his head in the door of Anna's room.

COMBET: Sweetheart. (*Moving into the room*) What are you doing awake?

ANNA: I wanted to say hello. I kept my school shoes on so I wouldn't get comfortable and go to sleep.

Combet pulls back the covers revealing her small feet still in their shoes. Still with their orthopaedic inserts.

I was determined.

Combet is suddenly awash with guilt.

COMBET: You go back to your mum's tomorrow, don't you?

He begins to unlace the shoes and pull them off.

You've hardly seen me this time ... Or the time before ... (*Sitting on the bed beside her, caressing her head*) How about I sit here while you go to sleep? I can read Tintin if you like.

ANNA: Can we just talk?

COMBET: Course. What would you like to talk about?

ANNA: I don't know. Nothing really.

They sit in silence for some time. Just being together. Anna's little hand sneaks out from under the bedclothes and takes his.

It's good you can make time for me, Dad.

She couldn't kick him harder in the guts if she tried.

SCENE 51. INT. THE HALLWAY AND KITCHEN – COMBET'S HOUSE. NIGHT.

Greg comes quietly out of Anna's room, pauses, and just leans against the wall. He stays like this for some moments until, eventually, Petra approaches from their bedroom. His body language tells her he's feeling lousy.

COMBET: I'll be in in a minute.

He turns away and walks to the kitchen. Petra follows him, and watches as he swings open the fridge door, assesses what's in there, and grabs a plate of leftover pasta or the like. He extracts a fork from a drawer and proceeds to eat. This provides him with no enjoyment, but he hasn't eaten since breakfast.

PETRA: That's got anchovies in it.
COMBET: No wonder it tastes like shit.

Petra says it as gently as she can – but she has to say it.

PETRA: You chose this, Greg. 'I'd lose a limb to run this thing.' Remember?

He knows. He remembers. What can he say?

A moment, then Petra moves forward and gives him the hug he so clearly, so desperately needs.

SCENE 52. INT. THE BEDROOM – JOSH'S FLAT. NIGHT.

It's very late. Josh is sitting in a chair in the corner of his bedroom, naked, going through an immense pile of legal documents by the light of a small lamp. He's tense, frustrated.

He looks up to where Tali sleeps in his bed, her back to him. He can see her shoulder and the ridge of her spine. He wants to be lying beside her, to touch her. But the work has to be done …

Finally he stands, moves quietly to the bed and leans across it, gently touching her back and shoulder, speaking softly. She does not wake.

JOSH: It's synchronicity. That the two most important things in my life have happened at exactly the same time.

He watches her breathing.

I'll take you to Randwick. You'll come round. I'll even take you to Ascot. It's not that I can't fly. It's just that I get this dry-mouth, sweaty-palm thing. I have been known to throw up. 'Sjust terror. Funny thing, though – tonight. Tonight you made me fly. And I was right as rain.

SCENE 53. INT./EXT. SEAN'S CAR – SUBURBAN STREET. DAY.

It is late March. Sean is driving slowly along a leafy suburban street, obviously looking for something. He talks into his mobile.

SEAN: Greg. Sean McSwain. We've got something. I've had a call from one of the scabs. He's willing to talk ... Mate, I think you'd better hear it for yourself ...

Dan Brodie appears from a clump of bushes and sprints towards the car.

DAN: You Sean?

SEAN: Yep.

Dan leaps into the car, slams the door shut and sinks down out of sight.

DAN: Get me out of here.

SCENE 54. INT. MUA WEST MELBOURNE OFFICE. DAY.

Dan Brodie's face. It is red and swollen from many tears. He is frightened and erratic. Josh, Greg and Sean are going over and over his story, testing it, checking his credibility as a witness.

DAN: I already told them everything I know.

COMBET: Tell us again.

DAN: Patrick's are going to sack all their blokes over Easter. They're training us to take over. Can I call my wife now?

COMBET: What do you mean all their blokes? All what blokes?

DAN: The blokes in the union.

COMBET: Where? Here?

DAN: Everywhere. Whole country.

COMBET: Every port in the country?

DAN: That's what I said.

COMBET: Patrick's are planning to sack every one of their union workers in every port in the country?

DAN: That's what I fuckin' said.

Combet, Josh and Sean catch their breath. This is the confirmation they've been looking for.

JOSH: Would you be prepared to say this on television?

DAN: Yes. No. I dunno. I have to talk to my wife. What am I going to say to her?

SEAN: Maybe you could tell her that being a scab's not all it's cracked up to be.

Josh shoots him a warning glance.

JOSH: Why have you come forward now?

DAN: 'Cos they're pricks. They treat you like shit. Promise you the world, then treat you like shit.

COMBET: In what way?

DAN: Phone bill.

JOSH: What?

DAN: They wouldn't pay my phone bill. And the TV. Well, I can't pay the fuckin' thing. I've got a wife and two-and-a-half kids to support. It was two grand.

JOSH: Two grand?

But Sean is smiling grimly.

SEAN: You've been racking up debts on the porn channel, haven't you, Danny boy?

The three union men exchange glances. Josh puts it into words.

JOSH: Well, that'll make for a credible witness.

COMBET: Who told you about the plan to sack the workforce?

JOSH: What exactly did they say?

DAN: The blokes at Webb Dock. The trainer blokes for the Farmers' Federation. They kept saying 'The shit's going to hit the fan at Easter'.

Dan finally loses it now and puts his head down and sobs.

She'll leave me. She'll leave me and she'll take the kids. She always said I was a no-hoper. This was my one chance to prove I could earn some decent money and look after 'em. And I've fucked it up ...

Sean's face. And suddenly there's some sympathy for this poor, messed up 'scab'.

SCENE 55. INT. COMMERCIAL TV STUDIO. DAY.

Josh and Combet stand in the background as Dan is hooked up to a radio microphone, his hair tidied and make-up applied to his face.

INTERVIEWER: Okay, Dan. We've got your wife standing by in Toowoomba.

DAN: What am I going to say to her?

He's a complete wreck. Josh and Combet exchange glances.

A voice comes from the darkness of the studio: 'Toowoomba's on line'.

And on the monitor appears Dan's young wife, nursing a young child, and clearly pregnant with another.

Hi, Mandy ...

MANDY: Am I on tele?

INTERVIEWER: No, not yet, we're just setting up. You can talk freely to your husband if you want to.

DAN: Hey, babe ...

MANDY: You fuckwit, Dan. You're piss weak. Things go well for a change, and just, typical, you have to go and fuck it up. Sometimes I think you're not right in the head, Dan Brodie. Sometimes I really think you're some kind of mongo.

Combet and Josh. Disaster in the making. Too late to do anything.

JOSH:Oh, God. I can't watch ...

The voice, off: 'Ten seconds to air. Ready everyone. Ten' ... 'three, two, one ...'

The interviewer faces the camera.

INTERVIEWER: Good evening, viewers. Tonight we have the extraordinary allegations of Dan Brodie, a young trainee stevedore with the National Farmers' Federation's new stevedoring arm. Dan has made the astonishing claim that the managing director of Patrick stevedores, Chris Corrigan, is planning to sack his entire workforce and replace them with ...

The interviewer continues the introduction as Combet and Josh mutter.

COMBET: This is driving me crazy.

JOSH: Uh?

COMBET: How? He can't sack two thousand people without being hit with an unfair-dismissal case? He can have redundancies, sure. But he can't sack the lot unless he closes down the business ...

JOSH: Maybe that's what he's doing.

COMBET: Not Corrigan. There's too much money to be made.

The interview continues ...

DAN: I just got tired of keeping it all secret, sneaking on and off the docks, having to be scared all the time. I thought, it's not right. What I'm saying's true. That's why they don't want me to say it ...

Combet and Josh. God – he's pulling it off.

INTERVIEWER: And we have Dan's wife standing by in Toowoomba. Dan says he fled unemployment in Queensland to take this job in order to support his young family. But his new bosses are calling him a liar and a cheat. What do you say to that, Mandy?

And butter couldn't melt in Mandy's mouth. She jiggles the baby appealingly on her lap.

MANDY: All I can say is this: I've loved Dan Brodie since the first moment I saw him. If he was any of those things you said, I never could've loved him. I never could have married him.

Combet and Josh. Maybe there is a God.

SCENE 56. INT. RECEPTION – COMMERCIAL TV STUDIO. NIGHT.

Sean is waiting when Dan walks out, flanked by Josh and Combet. Perhaps Sean slips a hip flask into his top pocket.

SEAN: Come on, Danny Boy. I'll get you home.

DAN: I'm not going back to that hotel. They'll kill me.

SEAN: It's okay, mate. We'll put you somewhere safe tonight, and get you home to Toowoomba tomorrow.

He is almost solicitous in his handling of Dan.

DAN: Think I've fucked my marriage.

SEAN: Nah, mate. It'll be right. You wait.

He lays the lightest of hands on Dan's shoulder, then removes it and shepherds the young man towards the door. Josh and Combet are silent observers of his compassion.

SCENE 57. EXT. SEAN'S HORSE FLOAT – WEBB DOCK. DAY.

It is early morning. The first autumn mist hovers in the air. A sense of unease, apprehension …

Sean is asleep in his horse float. His mobile phone is ringing. He drags himself from a deep sleep and grabs it.

SEAN: Hello …

GARY: Sean?

SEAN: Yeah?

GARY: Mate, it's Gary Welsh.

SEAN: Uh? Who?

GARY: The manager at Webb. If you look across to the tower you can probably see me. I'll get sacked if they find out I've talked to you. Mate, that kid on the tele last night. He's right.

Sean is instantly alert and concentrating.

SCENE 58. INT. THE MEETING ROOM – MAURICE, BLACKBURN, CASHMAN. DAY.

Josh, Coombs, Combet, Sean, Burnside and one or two other lawyers are assembled for a 'crisis meeting'. Everyone's a bit hot under the collar. Everyone, that is, except Burnside, who sits to one side, very quietly, taking it all in.

Sean is feeling pretty out of his depth in this company.

JOSH: This is a crisis, folks. It's ten days 'til Easter and all we've got is rumour and hearsay.

COMBET: Can't we injunct him against sacking his workforce?

JOSH: We haven't got enough to stand up in court. We've got Brodie – worse than useless in a court of law. And we've got your manager.

SEAN: He's a decent bloke. He's not bullshitting.

JOSH: I need him on the record. I need an affidavit from him. I need him in court.

SEAN: I said I wouldn't give him up. He'll lose his job.

JOSH: If we don't get this up, in ten days your entire membership are going to lose their jobs.

COOMBS: Son, once they're outside the gates we're going to have a bastard of a time getting 'em back in.

JOSH: Once they're outside the gates, we might have no chance at all of getting them back in. Bang goes the MUA.

Sean hesitates. For a long time.

SEAN: I'm sorry; I can't have him named.

A moment of white-knuckled silence.

JOSH: Could I have a quick word with you outside, mate?

Sean nods, and follows Josh out into the corridor.

SCENE 59. INT. OUTSIDE THE MEETING ROOM – MAURICE, BLACKBURN, CASHMAN. DAY.

Josh turns on Sean.

JOSH: Are you out of your fucking mind? You mightn't be quite across this yet, but this thing is bigger than one manager and one miserable job. It's bigger than one trade union …

SCENE 60. INT. THE MEETING ROOM – MAURICE, BLACKBURN, CASHMAN. DAY.

Silence in the meeting room, everyone pretending that they can't hear what's going on.

JOSH: *(out of view, muffled)* ... This is the thin end of the wedge for the whole labour movement, can't you see that? Are you a complete fucking dropkick?

A mumbled reply from Sean. An expletive from Josh, and after some moments, a falsely bright Josh reappears in the room, followed by Sean.

Any progress?

Combet shrugs. An awkward silence.

BURNSIDE: Look, I'm sorry I can't stay any longer. I've got a Chunky Move board meeting.

COOMBS: What in blazes is Chunky Move?

BURNSIDE: They're a local dance group. Contemporary dance. They're very good.

He's putting documents in his briefcase, preparing to leave.

That thought of yours earlier, Josh. What would happen if the workers were all sacked?

JOSH: They'd be reinstated.

BURNSIDE: Any exceptions?

JOSH: If the company's going out of business.

BURNSIDE: To do that, they'd have to dispose of their assets.

JOSH: Correct.

BURNSIDE: All right. John Coombs writes a letter to Chris Corrigan asking him to deny the rumours and to guarantee that, A, he won't dismiss the workforce and, B, he won't dispose of any assets. If he waffles around it, then I think we'll have just enough. Have you got a minute?

Josh, more than a bit sheepish, turns to follow Burnside out.

JOSH: Told you he was a genius.

SCENE 61. INT. OUTSIDE THE MEETING ROOM – MAURICE, BLACKBURN, CASHMAN. DAY.

A rather shamefaced Josh follows Burnside into the corridor.

BURNSIDE: In my experience in the law, I've found it necessary to moderate the influences of ideology and passion. They tend to obscure the process of rational thought. If you want this union to survive, and win, Josh, wrestle with the passion.

He smiles at Josh and goes on his way.

SCENE 62. EXT. WEBB DOCK. DUSK.

It is just on sunset. The protest gathered at Webb Dock is settling down for the night. Twenty-four gallon drums are being used as barbecues and heaters. Hot dogs are being cooked, smoke rising into the evening air. There's an odd sense of peace and community among those gathered, a sense of common cause, united as they are in the first autumn chill. It is strangely beautiful.

Josh walks along, incongruous in his suit, looking at the faces of the men and women he now officially represents. He doesn't belong here – but he so much wants to.

He spins as he hears a voice behind him.

SEAN: G'day.

JOSH: Uh ... Hey.

There's some awkwardness between them after the brawl in Josh's office.

SEAN: Want to see where I hang out?

He leads Josh to the Bermagui Belle horse float.

JOSH: Bugger me. Bermagui Belle. I won fifty bucks on her.

SEAN: No shit?

JOSH: She's a champ. Came from behind and won by half a length with a hairline fracture in her fetlock and a jockey with a thyroid problem.

Sean laughs. They settle onto the step of the horse float and look around at the other protesters.

John Coombs'd spew if he knew I was here.

SEAN: Yeah? He'd spew if he thought I wasn't.

JOSH: How many nights've you been here?

SEAN: Fifty-nine. And counting.

JOSH: Must be popular at home. You got kids?

SEAN: Two.

JOSH: Can they visit?
SEAN: My wife left me.
JOSH: Oh.

A particular penny drops for Josh.

Aaah ...

SEAN: Huh?

JOSH: The scab. Brodie. We thought you were going to eat his entrails. And you treated him like your long-lost brother.

Sean half smiles in acknowledgement. They sit in silence.

SEAN: Sometimes I feel like eating someone's entrails. Corrigan, or Reith, or that scab up there in my crane. All this control, this ... layer ... of civility we invented to stop us killing each other, reckon it drives men mad. See Podge over there?

He gestures to where Podge is hitting golf balls, one after the other, hard, over the fence at the security guards.

Sometimes I think his way of doing it might've been better: beat the crap out of each other and see who's left standing.

JOSH: Lawyers aren't encouraged to eat entrails. 'Cept in 'billable units'.

SEAN: Yeah. Well you did a pretty good impression of it this afternoon.

JOSH: Ah. Sorry about that.

SEAN: Forget it. Good to see a bloke in a suit with some blood in his veins.

SCENE 63. INT. THE LIVING ROOM – JOSH'S FLAT. NIGHT.

The news is on. Josh is tidying the flat, pushing untidy bits of newspaper and legal files and general refuse away under furniture and so on. On the television are images of Webb Dock, interviews with wharfies and their wives (ideally real footage). Josh is startled to find tears in his eyes.

A knock on the door. He rapidly wipes his eyes and opens the door to Tali.

JOSH: Hi.

TALI: Uh-oh.

She's heard the flatness in his tone.

JOSH: Sorry. Day from hell.

Her eye falls on the television. Together they watch for a moment. And Josh is tearing up again as he watches.

Oh, God, this is embarrassing. Come over, he says, I'll cook for you, wine and dine and seduce you. And here I am ... (*'close to awash.'*)

TALI: Start as you mean to go on, I guess.

Silence for a moment. Tali waits while he tries to find the words to express his feelings.

JOSH: Occurs to me that I haven't really moved far from my roots. Middle-class boy, middle-class degree, middle-class law firm.

TALI: Nice Jewish girlfriend.

JOSH: What can I possibly know about what those men are going through? All the education, all the privilege, only means something if it can help them. If the law can't deliver justice, then what the fuck am I doing here? What are any of us doing here?

TALI: Do you want me to go?

JOSH: No. Fuck, no.

Tonight is important to him.

I'm scared, that's all. I'm shit-scared I've promised them something I can't deliver.

SCENE 64. INT. COMBET'S OFFICE – ACTU. NIGHT.

Combet is at his desk, ploughing through the mountain in his 'in' tray while talking to Anna on the phone.

COMBET: ... Did you? Maybe you should ask Petra to put a bandaid on it ... Okay. Don't stay awake for me, huh? You get to sleep and I'll see you in the morning. I love you, sweetheart.

As he hangs up he hears that the fax machine outside his office has sprung to life. He rubs his tired eyes and gets up to investigate.

SCENE 65. INT. THE LIVING ROOM – JOSH'S FLAT. NIGHT.

Josh and Tali have finished dinner and are sitting very close, nursing glasses of wine. Perhaps Josh touches her face as he speaks. He seems nervous.

JOSH: Burnside gave me some very Burnside-like advice today. He told me to wrestle with my passions.

TALI: Can I watch?

JOSH: The twenty-four hour rule: let twenty-four hours pass before you respond to any impulse. That's what I should do. But the impulse to say this is kind of overwhelming ... I think I'm falling in love with you.

TALI: You're not promising something you can't deliver?

JOSH: Oh, man, I hope not. I fucking hope not.

SCENE 66. INT. RECEPTION – ACTU. NIGHT.

Documents are still spewing out of the fax machine. Combet is looking through them, totally gob-smacked. The words 'Cabinet in Confidence' appear on several of them. And the words 'Waterfront Strategy' on others. And he's already moving as he presses a number on his mobile.

COMBET: Josh? You awake? You are not going to believe this, mate. Can I come over?

SCENE 67. INT. THE LIVING ROOM – JOSH'S FLAT. NIGHT.

Documents on the table. Combet's hands, then Josh's turning them.

JOSH: Holy fuck ...

His hands are shaking.

Look at that. Look ... my hands are shaking ...

The two men, a glass of wine each, are going through the documents as though they are secret treasure – which, of course, they are.

There is no sign of Tali and Josh looks as though he might have dressed hastily.

JOSH: There's no fax number on them?

COMBET: Nothing. Just came through the machine, no cover, no identification. Nothing. Are they legit?

JOSH: Forgeries?

COMBET: It's been known to happen.

JOSH: Yeah, sure. Could be. But if they're not ... this is Howard's signature. On a document that authorises – what is it? – 'the interventionist strategy on the waterfront'. The Prime Minister's signature.

COMBET: Doesn't link him to Corrigan, though, does it?

JOSH: Not yet. But we'll find it. Do you know what this means?

COMBET: (*dry as toast*) We might have enough?

JOSH: This means we could bring the government down.

He's brimming with excitement like a small kid, trying to control it, unable to keep still, starting to do a restless, hopping kind of dance.

Shit. Calm calm calm. Twenty-four hour rule, Josh. (*Giving in*) We could bring the government down. Greg. We could bring the government down.

Combet's wry smile starts to emerge. Once more, against all his own instincts, he is infected by Josh's excitement.

COMBET: Is there any point telling you to settle?

Tali comes in from the bedroom, tousled, sleepy.

JOSH: Tali, meet Greg. Greg, Tali. I'm in love with her.

COMBET: Congratulations.

JOSH: Greg and I are going to bring down the government. What do you think of that?

He grabs Tali and begins to dance her around the room. Combet is laughing. Tali is laughing. It's an outburst of sheer, childlike, joyous excitement.

SCENE 68. INT./EXT. CORRIGAN'S OFFICE – PATRICK HEAD OFFICE. DAY.

Through the window of Corrigan's Kent Street office, Corrigan, helmet still in hand, listens to what Paul is telling him. Over this, the ABC's AM *radio programme:*

RADIO REPORTER: (*voice over*) You've been saying for some time that you think there's some sort of unholy conspiracy going on.

COOMBS: (*voice over*) Too right I have. We now have indisputable proof that this thing goes all the way to the upper echelons of the government.

SCENE 69. INT. CORRIGAN'S OFFICE – PATRICK HEAD OFFICE. DAY.

It is April 6th, 1998.

PAUL: They've lodged an application for an injunction to stop you dismissing the workforce.

CORRIGAN: Which court?

PAUL: Federal.

CORRIGAN: (*rolling his eyes*) Of course.

PAUL: It's going to be heard on Wednesday. Day after tomorrow.

CORRIGAN: Shit.

He breathes slowly, calmly, staying rational.

If we lose this chance we'll never get it again. We'll be stuck in this fucking quagmire for another fifteen years.

PAUL: And the rest.

CORRIGAN: There's no option. We'll have to move it forward.

PAUL: Are we ready?

CORRIGAN: We'll have to be.

PAUL: Chris. This is going to get really ugly.

CORRIGAN: I know that.

PAUL: I mean really ugly. The boss of the Chubb team told me, in his estimation, there's about a fifty percent chance of you coming out of it alive.

CORRIGAN: I'd appreciate it if you didn't repeat that to Valerie. She and Joe fly out this afternoon.

PAUL: And ... uh ... I have to ask this 'cos I'm the mug who's going to have to spin it. The dogs?

CORRIGAN: I said I didn't want them. They said there's no choice. If the wharfies decide to trash the sites, they haven't got enough men to stop them. Those cranes take six months to repair – if they're down that long the whole plan'll collapse.

And then he starts to smile, and suddenly snorts with laughter.

Fifty per cent chance, huh? So, what'll it be – Johnny Coombs coming at me with a six gun? (*Going to the window*) Actually, I'd quite enjoy that.

He looks down towards Darling Harbour, his face a mixture of apprehension, nerves, and sheer steely determination.

Bring it on.

His eye line travels down to the docks.

SCENE 70. EXT. DARLING HARBOUR. DAY.

Travelling from Corrigan's window down towards Darling Harbour. The image slows, darkens ...

SCENE 71. EXT. A DOCK. NIGHT.

Until it is night.

It is not Darling Harbour. It could be any dock in the country. It is working normally. But there is a sense that all is not as it seems ...

It is autumn. There is a faint mist in the air.

SCENE 72. EXT. A RIVER. NIGHT.

A dozen or so dinghies move silently up the river towards the well-lit port area at the end. On the dinghies are men wearing black trousers, white shirts and black ties. Some wear peaked caps. They hold large black Rottweiler dogs on leashes. The dogs sniff the mist that hovers over the water.

Super caption: '11.30 p.m. Tuesday April 7th, 1998'.

SCENE 73. EXT. MONTAGE. NIGHT.

And the scene stylises into a sequence that suggests identical activity at every port in the country.

Super caption: 'Brisbane'.

A man's hand clutching hard to a baton – a 'shit stick', as it will become known.

Super caption: 'Fremantle'.

The landing vessel splashing gently through the water.

Super caption: 'Newcastle'.

Boots, gently pacing, warming cold feet, readying them for action.

Super caption: 'Darling Harbour, Sydney'.

Boats nudging up against the wharves.

Super caption: 'East Swanston, Melbourne'.

Men clambering over the sides of the landing craft, moving at speed. It might almost be the D-Day landings.

Super caption: 'Port Botany, Sydney'.

A blur of rapid movement. Shouts. Men moving quickly, jumping, running. The alert face and slavering mouth of a Rottweiler.

Super caption: 'Webb Dock, Melbourne'.

Freeze frame on the face of the dog. And fade slowly to black.

END OF PART TWO

Sean's war: Sean McSwain (Anthony Hayes) on the docks.

SCENE 1. INT. LIMBO. DAY.

Sean McSwain addresses the camera.

SEAN: You can grow accustomed to sleeping in a horse float. Breathing in that fleshy, equine kind of smell. Knowing every time you walk out on a picket you stink of ... well ... horse.

Super caption: 'Sean McSwain, official, Maritime Union of Australia'.

SCENE 2. EXT. A WHARF. NIGHT.

A row of dark trousers and boots assembling into what might be military formation.

Super caption: '9 p.m. Tuesday, April 7th, 1998'.

SCENE 3. EXT. WEBB DOCK. NIGHT.

A wide, wide shot. Sean walks along the dock fence line, past a few sleepy protestors. He gestures to them. 'Evening.' A quiet, still night. Mist in the air.

Sean's narration continues:

SEAN: (*voice over*) Easter, they'd been saying, it was supposed to happen. We were on alert. But Easter's still four days away. Normal night. Me and the lingering scent of Bermagui Belle.

SCENE 4. EXT. – THE WHARF. NIGHT.

Boots and black trousers climb into small, quiet vessels, leading dogs on leashes.

Super caption: '9.30 p.m. Tuesday April 7th, 1998'.

SCENE 5. INT./EXT. SEAN'S HORSE FLOAT – WEBB DOCK. NIGHT.

A small fire in a corrugated-iron drum. Sean feeds a lump of paper into it … a succession of writs forbidding him to appear at Webb Dock.

SEAN: (*voice over*) Stoking the home fires with Supreme Court injunctions. Normal night.

Inside the horse float Sean pulls off his boots. Wraps his jacket and a couple of blankets around him and clambers into his sleeping bag, fully clothed. Lying back, he pulls out his mobile phone and presses the menu. A name appears on the screen: 'Janine'. Sean's finger hovers over the 'Call' button. Should he call her? He decides against, flicks the phone off and lies back, eyes open, staring unseeing into the darkness.

BASTARD BOYS

PART THREE: SEAN'S WAR

SCENE 6. INT./EXT. MONTAGE. NIGHT.

A burst of uptempo music – ideally Edwin Starr's 1970 hit 'War': 'War … What is it good for? Absolutely nothing …'

A rapid succession of images, some of which are repeated, others completely fresh:

Black dogs and army boots sprinting across the dock.

Sean reaching out in the darkness to grab his ringing mobile phone.

A press release spewing out of a fax machine: Patrick announces company restructure. A journalist grabs it, mouths: 'Hey, look at this' …

Peter Reith in a corridor at Parliament House, addressing a small cluster of journalists:

REITH: Cabinet met for three hours earlier tonight to devise a scheme to finance the redundancies. Patrick has terminated its labour-hire contracts and replaced them with new contractors.

Brendan sliding down the final steps of his crane. He is surrounded by security men with batons and big black dogs. He is terrified.

Tony in his straddle, a look of madness on his face, wheeling the big machine, heading towards a cluster of security men and dogs. Through his walkie-talkie a voice is calling for calm.

TONY: Get fucked …

The head office of Patrick, high above Kent Street, Sydney. A cluster of company execs and security men watch images on a bank of video screens.

Greg Combet waking with a start, answering his ringing mobile, Petra bleary beside him.

John Coombs in a caravan, Gwen sleeping beside him, grabs his ringing mobile.

Josh Bornstein wakes abruptly, alone in his flat, and grabs the ringing phone.

Tight images of what might be riots: rocks, golf balls, one-inch nuts and beer stubbies thrown over cyclone wire fences; fences being shaken; angry faces shouting abuse; a key digging sharply into the big black hand of an Islander security guard, drawing blood …

Super captions: 'Newcastle' … 'Melbourne' … 'Sydney'… 'Brisbane' … 'Fremantle' …

A house in Point Piper is sprayed with paint. The word 'SCAB' and other obscenities being scrawled on the expensive walls …

Greg Combet fielding calls: 'This is disgraceful' … 'It is un-Australian' … 'I have one objective: to get every single one of these men back through those gates …'

And eventually:

SCENE 7. EXT. MAIN GATE – WEBB DOCK. PRE-DAWN.

All along the fence line of the docks are rows of wharfies, ugly-faced, screaming obscenities and abuse through the fence at security guards and the remaining managers. Some try to climb the fence. Some are throwing any kind of missile they can find: stones, pebbles, screws and bolts.

One security guard holds up a wad of cash several centimetres thick and waves it provocatively at the wharfies. The wharfies respond with renewed fury.

Sean is pushing his way through them, using his loudhailer when he can, but mostly just brute force and his voice, hauling them back, cautioning them. 'Stop. No violence. The strategy relies on there being no violence.' He encounters Tony Tully, in full flight, throwing stones, screaming. Sean pulls him back. Tony shrugs him off and moves forward again. Only fragments of the dialogue can be heard.

TONY: What bloody strategy?

SEAN: No violence, Tone. Don't you understand English?

TONY: Piss off. What else are we gunna do?

SEAN: Anybody caught using violence gets suspended from the Union. Get. Back.

TONY: Aaah. Bullshit ...

Sean really has his work cut out here.

SCENE 8. EXT. SEAN'S HORSE FLOAT – WEBB DOCK. PRE-DAWN.

Sean is behind his horse float, vomiting. He clutches an ageing sweat-stained paperback.

Brendan appears behind him and eases the book from his hand. It is an old Left Book Club edition of The Communist Manifesto.

BRENDAN: Bit bloody easier reading Karl and Fred than dealing with the real McCoy, eh?

SEAN: This is really volatile, mate. There's more arriving all the time. If I can't control them and there's bloodshed, we're fucked.

Brendan knows.

BRENDAN: Wanta know something? I've never been so scared in my life. I thought they were going to fuckin' kill me.

The mutual admission of fear and vulnerability draws the two closer together.

SCENE 9. INT / EXT. COOMBS' CAR – FREEWAY. PRE-DAWN.

A grim-faced John Coombs is driving himself and Gwen back to Sydney from their farm. On the car radio is one of the infamous Sydney shock jocks. Coombs has his mobile phone to his ear, waiting to be connected.

MORNING SHOCK JOCK: (*on the radio*) ... so they've got three blokes to man two cranes, okay, turn and turn about? So what do our noble working-class friends, the wharfies, do? Two blokes do the gig, the other nicks off for the arvo. And this productive little custom is so enshrined it's even got a nickname. That's it – they call it 'the nick'. It's a wonder Chris Corrigan didn't lock 'em out years ago.

Coombs gets through.

COOMBS: This is John Coombs ... I want to talk to –

MORNING SHOCK JOCK: Well, well, well. The man himself. John Coombs, head banana of the wharfies. Tell us about the nick, John.

COOMBS: What I'll tell you about, Richard, is a despicable, underhand, duplicitous deal between Chris Corrigan and Peter Reith to throw two thousand working people on the scrap heap ... and I'll tell you something else for free, Richard. It will not stand.

SCENE 10. EXT. CORRIGAN'S HOUSE – POINT PIPER. DAY.

Chris Corrigan is driven from the underground car park up the drive and out the gate. He sees his neighbour, the Spanish Consul, standing on the nature strip in front of his residence. He is still in pyjamas and looking very bewildered.

Corrigan addresses him out the car window.

CORRIGAN: Morning, Carlos.

CARLOS: Chris. Something unusual seems to have happened.

Corrigan climbs from the car, followed by Claude. The walls of the consulate building are splattered with red paint. Daubed over and over again is the word 'SCAB', along with other obscenities.

Corrigan glances at Claude. Then turns back to Carlos, his mouth dry.

CORRIGAN: Oh, those Basque separatists. Give them an inch ...

The joke dies a death.

CARLOS: But these are not Spanish words, I think.

An awful hiatus. Claude murmurs to Corrigan.

CLAUDE: We changed the house numbers around.

CORRIGAN: (*to Carlos*) I'll arrange to have it cleaned, Carlos. Go back to bed.

SCENE 11. INT. THE BOARDROOM – PATRICK HEAD OFFICE. DAY.

The room is packed with journalists, microphones and cameras.

SCENE 12. INT. OUTSIDE THE BOARDROOM – PATRICK HEAD OFFICE. DAY.

Corrigan stands outside, waiting. He gives Paul a quick, nervous smile, squares his shoulders, and walks into the full glare of the cameras.

SCENE 13. INT. THE BOARDROOM – PATRICK HEAD OFFICE. DAY.

Questions are shouted at him. The one he registers most clearly is: 'How do you feel this morning, Mr Corrigan?'

CORRIGAN: I have ... ahm ... excuse me ... mixed emotions this morning. The actions we've been forced to take are legitimate, and will be for the benefit of the country. But I have a sense of genuine disappointment for my – my former employees because I think they have been, for years, betrayed by their own union.

SCENE 14. EXT. WEBB DOCK. DAY.

Sean directs a line of vehicles to prevent any movements in and out of the main gates. Only some of what he says can be made out.

SEAN: No trucks in. None out. Cargo stays on the docks.

He moves on past a member of the Electrical Workers Union, who is diverting electricity from a power pole down to a transformer on the ground, powering lights, a television set, and a couple of heaters.

Behind him several large men lever up a set of railway tracks and begin to weld them into strange and vaguely artistic shapes.

More and more people are arriving, and now the crowd parts to reveal a group of rather sassy young women walking through with a banner that reads 'Sex Workers for the Wharfies'. There's a round of applause.

A radio voice over accompanies these images:

REITH: (*voice over*) Today the Government has acted decisively to fix the waterfront once and for all. We believe that within a very short period of time – twelve to eighteen months – we will see a complete turnaround in the levels of productivity and reliability on the Australian waterfront …

A dreadlocked feral pulls down a sign that says 'Food, not Bombs' and replaces it with a sign that says 'Food, not Scabs'. Outside his tent are various pots and pans sitting atop a range of hotplates.

Sean wanders over.

FERAL: Breakfast, mate?

He sticks a filthy arm directly into one of his pots and stirs the food.

SEAN: Just a bit of fruit, thanks, mate.

From behind he hears his name and turns. A young process server has bailed up Brendan and Tony.

PROCESS SERVER: I'm looking for Sean McSwain. You can't tell me where he is, can you?

Brendan gestures with his head to Sean – be inconspicuous – as Tony answers the young man.

TONY: You a relative, are you, son?

PROCESS SERVER: No. Um. Just some documents I have to give him.

TONY: Sorry, mate. He was here a few minutes ago, but I think he went off somewhere. Bren?

BRENDAN: Yeah. Yeah, said he'd be gone for a while.

TONY: You can't miss him, though. Big boofy bloke. Mop of orange hair. I'll let him know you were looking for him.

PROCESS SERVER: (*dispirited*) Yeah. Thanks.

BRENDAN: There you go, matey.

He hands the hapless lad a handful of MUA stickers, and the process server wanders off with his tail between his legs. Sean gives a thank you gesture to the Tullys. A reminder that someone's on his side.

SCENE 15. EXT. FEDERAL COURT – MELBOURNE. DAY.

April 8th, 1998. Legal personnel, journalists and interested members of the public are scampering into the Federal Court as a journalist addresses camera.

FEMALE ABC JOURNALIST: The nation has awoken this morning to find that the goalposts in this dispute have been radically shifted. I'm here at the Federal Court where the Maritime Union is seeking an injunction to prevent Chris Corrigan from sacking his workers. But in last night's coup on the docks, it looks as though Corrigan may have stolen the march on them …

SCENE 16. INT. FEDERAL COURT – MELBOURNE. DAY.

Tension is high in the court as Josh Bornstein leads Julian Burnside and the rest of his legal team into court. Stuart, one of the juniors on the Patrick legal team, does a double take.

STUART: Fuck me senseless. They've got Burnside.

Josh need not hear this – the look on Stuart's face is enough to make his day.

JOSH: Morning, Stuart.

And then:

The MUA team are just getting settled at the bar table when the head of the Patrick legal team, John Middleton, leans across and hands Burnside a sheaf of documents.

MIDDLETON: Bit of a shift in the rules of engagement, Julian. The four labour companies have been put into voluntary administration.

BURNSIDE: Labour companies?

MIDDLETON: The companies that employ the men. Completely separate from the parent company.

JOSH: Since when?

MIDDLETON: Patrick restructured last year, I believe.

This is a total ambush.

Greg Combet and John Coombs, sitting in the front row, are leaning forward to hear this. Combet pales. So does Josh.

JOSH: Oh, fuck ... It's an ambush ...

And for Combet, months of puzzlement have been resolved.

COMBET: So that's how he's done it. Fuck. *Why didn't I spot it?*

COOMBS: What?

COMBET: He's shifted all the money out of these companies so they provide the labour *only.* Then he's sent them broke. This is the filthiest piece of corporate skulduggery I've ever seen.

But Burnside looks up from the documents and just smiles.

BURNSIDE: This is bottom-of-the-harbour.

Josh doesn't get it.

They'll never get away with it. Judges don't like being played for suckers. Run and get me a copy of the Corporations Law, will you, Josh? Oh, and a can of Pepsi.

And the court stands as Justice North makes his way to the bench.

SCENE 17. INT. FEDERAL COURT – MELBOURNE. DAY.

Burnside is on his feet.

BURNSIDE: We are here, Your Honour, to apply merely for an injunction to prevent the dismissal of the workforce. And yet, before our very eyes, proof is emerging of the larger conspiracy, which we allege. It's interesting, isn't it, that the events of last night took place a mere twenty-four hours after we served motion seeking to prevent Patrick from doing the very thing they have just done. At eleven p.m. Mr Reith's office announces the appointment of administrators to Patrick. Not ten minutes later, Patrick announces the workers' termination, with redundancies funded by the government. Not ten minutes later. What a remarkable coincidence.

Dissolve to:

MIDDLETON: I don't know what happens if Your Honour makes the order, but, quite frankly, there's no money. Furthermore, the companies are no longer under the control of Mr Corrigan. It is up to the administrators to decide whether they should continue operating.

Dissolve to:

JUSTICE NORTH: It is difficult for me under the law to force an insolvent company to continue trading. Mr Burnside?

BURNSIDE: Your Honour. Unless this court grants an injunction to prevent the sacking of these workers then this conspiracy will be a fait accompli. And Patrick and the government will have proved that it's possible to get rid of a workforce, through no fault of their own, simply with a few strokes of a pen.

North pauses, looks to Middleton, back to Burnside. He is troubled.

NORTH: Thank you, Mr Burnside. I will adjourn for one hour and return with my decision.

SCENE 18. INT. THE MEETING ROOM – MAURICE, BLACKBURN, CASHMAN. DAY.

Josh walks into a meeting of the Maurice, Blackburn, Cashman partners. All faces turn to him. Well?

JOSH: We got it. Yeah, we got it. Stayed 'til after Easter. He'll hear the full case then. Yeah ...

And everybody in the room begins to applaud. Josh just stands there, his eyes filling with tears.

SCENE 19. EXT. FEDERAL COURT – MELBOURNE. DAY.

Julian Burnside leaves the court building and walks across its paved exterior. A couple of fellow barristers are hovering, glancing at legal briefs, chatting desultorily.

BARRISTER: Julian. What'd he do?

BURNSIDE: We got the order. A few days' grace.

The barristers give vague grunts and go back to their activities. A shadow of pain crosses Burnside's face, and then he walks away, thoughtful.

Julian Burnside, doyen of the corporate world, has crossed the line ...

SCENE 20. INT. THE BOARDROOM – MUA. DAY.

April 10th, 1998. A strategy meeting: Combet, Kelty, Coombs, Josh, Sean, Jennie George, a few other ACTU and MUA representatives. Combet chairs the meeting.

A television quietly burbles away in the background.

COMBET: ... First and foremost, we are not running pickets. Pickets are illegal. What's taking place on the docks is a series of spontaneous 'peaceful assemblies'. We can't stop Corrigan unloading cargo with scab labour ... but we can get a few hundred God-fearing citizens at the gates to exercise their democratic rights when he tries to move it through.

COOMBS: The Australian Endeavour's docking at Webb on Sunday. It's crewed by our members. I can't ask them to work beside scabs.

JOSH: No choice. We're gone for all money if you don't. Secondary boycott.

COMBET: Let them unload it, John. The pickets'll stop it getting through.

He looks around at the sea of faces, all eyes on his.

Did someone just say 'pickets'? That's a scandalous allegation ...

He grins. A moment of relieved tension.

Okay. There are three clear planks of this strategy: The legal approach. Contained industrial action. And winning the hearts and minds.

SEAN: Can I say something?

COMBET: Yep?

SEAN: Seems to me we're counting on two things: One. That none of the blokes takes the redundancy package – and it's a bloody good offer. Two. That we can hold discipline.

COOMBS: If they can see progress being made, they'll hold. I've never lost a bloke yet.

KELTY: (*to Coombs*) You still determined to keep P and O working?

COOMBS: I'd be mad if I didn't. We need them. Every one of those blokes is putting in a hundred quid a week so we can pay the Patrick blokes. But with fourteen hundred out, we're looking at four hundred grand a week. I need the other unions …

Combet notices Kelty's eyes moving from himself to Josh, and back. He knows Kelty is watching his strategic handling of the dispute.

COMBET: Did you want to say something, Bill?

KELTY: Nuh. No. Go on.

COMBET: You've got full ACTU backing on the money, John. That's a firm commitment. Okay, the PR angle on this is that the blokes are there, ready to walk in and work. No shorts and T-shirts. No booze …

Fade out as Combet continues his briefing. Coombs and Sean both know the pressure is on.

SCENE 21. INT. THE BOARDROOM – MUA. DAY.

Later. As the meeting breaks up and the assembled make their way out, Josh finds himself in front of the television. He turns the volume up. Combet joins him.

On the television Ray Martin is interviewing John Howard.

JOHN HOWARD: … Desperately need an efficient waterfront if we are to survive and prosper in the modern economic environment.

RAY MARTIN: If it was about productivity, then why sack waterfront workers in Adelaide and productive ports?

JOHN HOWARD: Well, they're all part of the one union. I mean we didn't sack them ...

RAY MARTIN: They had to go?

JOHN HOWARD: Look ... clearly the union had declared war on the company ...

JOSH: Conspiracy? What conspiracy?

SCENE 22. EXT. WEBB DOCK. DAY.

Sean is talking on his mobile phone.

SEAN: I know it's bloody Easter. I know he's home on holidays. But I'm stuck at the docks. Okay, Nicky's too young, fair enough. But if you don't want to bring Alex down, at least bring him to the MUA office. I can ... Oh, forget it. It's all too bloody hard, isn't it?

He severs the connection, pissed off.

SCENE 23. EXT. THE DRIVEWAY – HOTEL. NIGHT.

A van marked 'Executive Laundry Service' is pulled up in the drive. Eventually Chris Corrigan emerges from the hotel, stretching one long leg after the other. He carries a pile of plastic-covered suits and a suitcase. And wriggles his neck to try to correct the crick in his spine. Corrigan's principal security man follows him.

FRANK: ... And, under no circumstances, are you to step outside the building without at least one escort and before the camouflaged car is available ...

CORRIGAN: Camouflaged car?

The security man nods. That's right. And the penny drops for Corrigan. He turns to look again at the laundry van. This is it? The camouflaged car?

Corrigan involuntarily bursts out laughing. The security man looks wounded.

Yes. Sorry, Frank. I'm sure that's very suitable.

And he breaks up laughing again.

Church bells begin tolling. One church, then another, then another … Easter has arrived.

SCENE 24. EXT. WEBB DOCK. DAY.

Easter Sunday, April 12th, 1998. A priest or minister on a makeshift stage addresses the crowd through a microphone. Behind him are arrayed a collection of ministers of other Christian denominations.

MINISTER: Easter is the season of rebirth, renewal, reaffirmation of our enduring values. In a world increasingly dominated by the new religion of profit, perhaps we should take this opportunity to pledge ourselves once again to the values of community, of charity, of unselfishness; to the abiding principle of doing unto others as we would have them do unto us.

Sean stands with Greg Combet watching a news report on a television set up at the gates. The television is showing footage of a ship called the Australian Endeavour being stevedored in an Australian port. At the top of the screen is the word 'File'.

NEWSREADER: (*voice over*) … Australian Endeavour, shown here in file footage, belongs to the ANL line and is crewed by Maritime Union members. But this morning, at Webb Dock, it will be stevedored by non-union labour, in an attempt by Chris Corrigan's Patrick to prove that a stevedoring operation can continue functioning without union workers …

Over this:

SEAN: What are we endeavouring for, d'y'reckon? Not a fair society, that's for sure.

COMBET: We've got to start now. Convincing the men that this is the end of the world as they know it. If we can get 'em back in – *if* … they're going to have to make concessions. Going to be a brave new world, comrade.

SEAN: These blokes are not rocket scientists, Greg. They've never seen the MUA lose. Never even seen it compromise. Go gently, eh?

Combet is taken aback by this level of wisdom and compassion. But before he can pursue it, he turns to see his daughter Anna. Beside her is Yannis. And bringing up the rear is Petra. All three wear 'MUA HERE TO STAY' T-shirts.

The smile that lights up Greg's face could tear Sean's heart out – here is a man who is loved and supported by his family.

PETRA: We thought the mountain should come to Mohammed.

COMBET: Thanks.

PETRA: No need.

COMBET: Ah … Sean McSwain. My partner Petra. Anna. And Yannis.

ANNA: We're having a picnic.

SEAN: Good for you.

He gives Anna a wink and moves off. As he goes, he sees Greg put an arm around Petra and hug her, grateful that she's come.

Sean crosses to where the Tully family have made themselves comfortable. The Easter roast has been brought down, crockery, cutlery, decent chairs. The works. Tony and Lyn are there, Brendan, Cherie, a few other family members with their partners and kids. Lyn is carving an immense roast lamb.

LYN: Tony Tully misses out on the Easter roast for nobody.

TONY: Yeah … but he misses out on his Easter shandy for Chris Bloody Corrigan.

BRENDAN: Yeah, long time since you've looked an orange juice in the face, eh, old man? Hey, Sean. Come and get some lunch before lard-arse here scoffs the lot. There's enough, isn't there, Mum?

'Lard arse' is a reference to Cherie, who could not be less *lard-arsed if she tried. She is, in fact, a very beautiful young woman – and Brendan clearly adores her.*

Sean hovers on the edge of the group, out of place, uncertain. Cherie promptly hands him her own plate, which she has not yet started eating.

CHERIE: Here. You can't tell me with a name like 'Sean McSwain' you'd knock back a baked spud.

The Combet family. Left to right, Petra Hilsen (Lucy Bell), Yannis Hilsen (Kurtis Papadinis). Anna Combet (Joanna Hunt-Prokhovnik) and Greg Combet (Daniel Frederiksen) join the protest.

Sean stands, still uncertain.

SEAN: Ta.

Suddenly, from behind him, a ripple of voices. 'They're coming. The scabs are coming.'

TONY: Oh, wouldn't you bloody know it …

The 'scab' bus, its windows darkened, starts to make its way through the crowd. The crowd surrounds it, chanting once more: 'MUA, here to stay!'

SCENE 25. EXT. PATRICK'S MELBOURNE DOCK. DAY.

Corrigan, wearing a safety vest, is standing near the bow of a ship, as, behind him, cranes, manned by non-union labour, unload containers. There are cries of 'Scab' and other abuse from the crew of the ship but Corrigan ignores them.

CORRIGAN: It's fitting that this should be the name of the first ship we handle under the new system. Australian Endeavour – endeavouring for greater efficiency, higher productivity, the principle of a fair day's work for a fair day's pay. True competitiveness in the world environment, not lip service to outdated and suffocating rhetoric. That's my definition of 'Australian endeavour'.

A photographer busily snaps away.

A blast of dance music. Corrigan puts a hand up, shielding his eyes from the sun in an attempt to see what's going on outside the gates. He can't.

SCENE 26. EXT. WEBB DOCK. DAY.

The Sex Workers for the Wharfies begin to dance the Macarena. People watch in puzzlement. And then, in ones and twos, they begin to join in.

More and more join in.

Cherie drags Brendan up and together they do a very raunchy version of the Macarena, loins to loins, hips to hips.

Sean watches this with a wave of envy.

Petra laughs and takes the hands of both Anna and Yannis and they join in.

Lots of people dancing now, and the formation is starting to take shape. For a moment it starts to look like a musical ...

Tony Tully is sounding off to anyone who will listen.

TONY: They're our blokes – our fucking blokes – on that ship being unloaded by scabs. What does John Coombs think he's doing?

Back at the Macarena, Petra signals to Greg. Come on. Join in ... Combet waves this suggestion away. Once. And again: I am not *doing the Macarena. Then his face softens and, just for a moment, in solidarity, he waves a single arm in a Macarena gesture. Petra smiles.*

A news journo is standing in front of the dancing group, addressing a camera for the evening news. Combet and Sean pass behind her as she speaks.

FEMALE ABC JOURNALIST: ... Dispute has become a tug-of-war over public opinion. On the one hand this is an immense psychological victory for Chris Corrigan and the Government because, under the very nose of the Maritime Union, we're seeing a ship stevedored by non-union labour. But the sheer numbers turning up to support the wharfies suggest otherwise, and what Corrigan can't, of course, achieve, is any movement of cargo onto or away from the docks ...

Greg and Sean are only too aware of the delicate balance at stake here.

SCENE 27. INT./EXT. COMBET'S CAR – COMBET'S HOUSE. DAY.

The Combet car turns into the driveway. Combet is sunk in the deepest gloom. The kids are tired and a bit fractious in the back seat, squabbling over an Easter egg. It has been a silent trip home from the docks.

COMBET: Thanks for coming down today.

PETRA: I said: no need.

COMBET: Stop being so bloody German. It's polite to say thank you.

PETRA: Stop being so Australian.

COMBET: Right at the moment it's taking an immense effort to just maintain the basic courtesies. I don't want to fight about saying thank you.

PETRA: Oh, but I do. Off you go, kids.

The light bickering is beginning to develop the tiniest edge. The kids have sniffed conflict in the air and do not move.

COMBET: Pet. This is going to get a lot worse before it gets better. If it gets better.

A moment, while Petra thinks about which way to play it. Then:

PETRA: Then I'll try to remember my manners.

He knows she's taking the piss. But it's the circuit-breaker they both need. He is about to say 'Thank you', stops. Smiles. And opens the car door.

SCENE 28. EXT. WEBB DOCK. EVENING.

The afternoon is cooling off, and many have left. The Tully family are packing up to go home.

Cherie wanders over to Sean, who sits at the edge of his horse float arranging picket rosters on his mobile phone. He rings off as she approaches.

CHERIE: Hey there, Spud.

SEAN: Watch yourself. Lard arse.

Cherie holds up a handful of small Easter eggs.

CHERIE: We've got these left over. You've got a little boy, haven't you?

SEAN: That's good of you, mate. But I'm pretty much stuck here for the duration.

CHERIE: Bren and me'll drop them in on the way home. Where d'you live?

SEAN: Heidelberg.

CHERIE: Yeah, well. We'll go home the scenic route. Write him a note, and we'll drop them in.

Sean hesitates, then pulls an old shift roster from his pocket and begins to write: 'Hey, Alexander the Great ...'

And looks up.

SEAN: Thanks, mate. Appreciate it.

SCENE 29. EXT/INT. SEAN'S HORSE FLOAT – WEBB DOCK. NIGHT.

Sean comes in blowing on his cold hands. He picks up a texta and moves to the horse-float wall where he has stuck a kind of calendar on which he is numbering the days. He crosses out the number 72 and writes the number 73. 73 long, cold, lonely nights ...

Fade to black.

SCENE 30. INT. FEDERAL COURT – MELBOURNE. DAY.

April 14th, 1998. The court is packed to the rafters. Immense excitement and anticipation. There are at least six legal teams assembled representing the various interested parties.

A journalist addresses camera.

FEMALE ABC JOURNALIST: All eyes are on the Federal Court where today Justice North will begin to hear the MUA's full case for preventing Patrick sacking its workers ...

SCENE 31. INT. AN ANTECHAMBER – FEDERAL COURT. DAY.

Julian Burnside is alone. He is breathing deeply, quietly rearranging the sticky tabs on the pages of his legal documents. Pacing a couple of steps. Rearranging the tabs again. He is not nervous. This is simply his way of working towards the necessary level of concentration.

Josh enters and speaks very quietly as he lays a box containing three espresso coffees and three cans of Pepsi on the table.

JOSH: Here's your fix, Julian.

Burnside just nods and Josh quietly withdraws. As he is closing the door:

BURNSIDE: We're making history, Josh.

SCENE 32. INT. A CORRIDOR – FEDERAL COURT. DAY.

Burnside joins Josh, Coombs and Combet.

BURNSIDE: You do all realise that if we lose this, you'll probably get costs and damages?

A glance between Coombs and Combet.

COMBET: What's the MUA worth?

COOMBS: Nineteen million. Give or take.

BURNSIDE: I don't think that'll quite cover it. Patrick, the NFF, the Government ... We're looking at several hundred million, I would think.

Both Coombs and Combet look like they could vomit. A long silence, then:

COOMBS: Oh, well, we're stuffed whichever way we go, then.

SCENE 33. INT. FEDERAL COURT – MELBOURNE. DAY.

Burnside addresses the court.

BURNSIDE: Your Honour. This story has all the hallmarks of a Robert Ludlum page-turner. And the more pages you turn, the deeper and more contrived and – dare I say it – the more sinister this conspiracy becomes ...

SCENE 34. INT. PATRICK HEAD OFFICE. DAY.

Closed-circuit television shows images from the docks: Sean coaching the protestors in passive resistance – linking arms with the person beside them, and holding the belt of the one in front. There's a glimpse of a group of police, apparently assembling. Corrigan and Paul are watching. On the bank of screens they can see what is happening on all the Patrick docks in the country.

CORRIGAN: They want to go us for conspiracy. It's hilarious. If we were in a conspiracy, how did we get ourselves in such a bloody mess?

PAUL: When there's a choice between conspiracy and cock-up, my money's on cock-up.

Corrigan is frustrated. He gestures at images coming in from a Sydney dock.

CORRIGAN: Look at this. The police are doing the bloody macaroni on the picket lines.

PAUL: Macarena.

CORRIGAN: Thank you. Why aren't they moving them? Why can't I get a message out that explains my side of this bloody thing?

PAUL: You've got to admit, Chris, Rotties on the docks is not a good look.

He holds up an MUA poster which features a balaclavaed security guard sitting in a bus shelter. See what we're up against?

Corrigan looks from the poster to Paul.

CORRIGAN: Have you been moonlighting again?

He starts to pace.

I didn't want the dogs. I told them I didn't want them. Anyway, did anyone get bitten by a dog? Are we being taken to court for teeth marks? No. And did the dogs make the threatening phone calls? Shout the obscenities? The nails under car tyres? The slingshots over the fences? Did the dogs chuck cups of urine in people's faces? No.

PAUL: One fell overboard. Technically that's water pollution.

CORRIGAN: This is a bloody farce.

He stops. Draws breath. And his naturally dry sense of humour reasserts itself.

Do you reckon you could train Rottweilers to drive cranes? I'd save a bloody fortune.

SCENE 35. INT. THE ANTECHAMBER – FEDERAL COURT. DAY.

Burnside, Josh, Coombs and Combet.

BURNSIDE: This is 'Spot the deliberate mistake', I'm afraid. We don't want to bring the company down, we want our jobs back. That's why we're allowing the company's entire cargo to rot on the docks. You see my problem? It would make my life a lot easier in there if we could just make the pickets go away for a few days.

Coombs looks apoplectic. Josh leaps into damage control.

JOSH: Thanks, Julian. I think it's going pretty well, all things considered. If I could just have a quick word with Greg and John ... ?

Burnside nods and withdraws. Coombs holds his breath just long enough.

COOMBS: Is he certifiable? 'Just make the pickets go away'. What fucking planet is he on?

COMBET: John, mate ...

JOSH: Look. Okay. Okay. He's not one of us. He doesn't understand about the noble struggle and all that. But he's the best, John. You've got to trust me.

Coombs looks daggers at him.

SCENE 36. EXT. MAIN GATE – WEBB DOCK. DAY.

Hard cut to a line of police trying to move the protestors. Sean is leading the protestors in passive resistance, chanting loudly: 'MUA, here to stay'.

Above: Easter lunch at the docks: Lyn Tully (Michele Fawdon), Tony Tully (Jack Thompson), Sean McSwain (Anthony Hayes), Brendan Tully (Daniel Wyllie) and Cherie Snape (Anna Lise Phillips). Below: protesting on the wharf.

Television cameras are taking it all in.

Messy, moving images. Until a single camera moves closer and closer in, to the faces of two little girls. Their father is on the ground. They crouch in his lap for protection, as the police move in, trying to pull the protestors away. The two little girls are clearly distressed.

Moving closer still into their terrified faces ...

SCENE 37. INT. THE LIVING ROOM – SEAN'S HOUSE. DAY.

Janine is in her nurse's uniform, hurrying around collecting clothes, shoes and toys.

Alex stands in front of the television in the lounge room. His face is blotched with chocolate from the Easter egg he's eating – one of those sent by Sean.

JANINE: Alex, will you turn that off and get whatever toys you want? I don't want to be here any longer than ...

She stops. On the television, the terrified little girls on the picket line.

ALEX: I saw Dad ...

Janine watches the television, troubled.

SCENE 38. INT. PATRICK HEAD OFFICE. DAY.

Corrigan turns away from the television where the same images are playing.

CORRIGAN: Oh, Christ. This is a disaster ...

Paul puts his hand over the mouthpiece of his phone – he's fielding media calls.

PAUL: You're kidding, aren't you? It's fucking great.

SCENE 39. INT. A CORRIDOR – FEDERAL COURT. DAY.

John Coombs is pacing, snapping into his mobile phone.

COOMBS: ... It's on the news, all over the fucking country. Kids. Scared bloody witless. What in the name of God do you think you're doing? What's Mum of Carlingford going to make of that, huh?

SCENE 40. EXT. MAIN GATE – WEBB DOCK. DAY.

Sean, on his mobile phone, cops this drubbing from the boss.

SEAN: The wife's working. He's rostered on the picket. Someone's got to mind the kids ... I didn't know – (*'the cops'd come today ...'*)

SCENE 41. INT. A CORRIDOR – FEDERAL COURT. DAY.

COOMBS: Yeah, well, next time you do know. You know every single picture those cameras are getting.

SEAN: (*on the phone*) I thought the family was meant to be the backbone of the union movement –

COOMBS: If you're not up to this, son, you better say so now. Channel Nine doesn't take prisoners, y'know. I can't put excuses on Ray Bloody Martin.

SEAN: (*on the phone*) We've been talking about getting a crèche going ...

COOMBS: Maybe you oughta throw yourself under a truck to distract 'em. Bloody dispute'd be over if you got yourself killed.

He rings off.

SCENE 42. EXT. MAIN GATE – WEBB DOCK. DAY.

Sean, his collar hunched against the cold, clicks off his mobile.

SEAN: Thanks for the support, comrade.

SCENE 43. INT. SEAN'S HORSE FLOAT – WEBB DOCK. NIGHT.

It's cold. And Sean feels lousy. He crosses out the number 75. And writes the number 76.

He hears a tap on the wall and turns. It's Brendan, pulling a neatly rolled joint from behind his ear and holding it up. Interested?

SEAN: (*tempted*) You motherless prick ...

BRENDAN: All right. So go the Clinton. Don't inhale. Mac, you're never going to get the real bad-heads to follow you into the trenches if you don't loosen up a bit.

SEAN: I thought you thought unions were for the birds?

BRENDAN: Yeah. But I can't let Cherie find that out. Wouldn't get my end in for a month. She's rabid, mate.

A grin and a wink. If he is changing his position, he's not going to admit it.

SCENE 44. INT./EXT. SEAN'S HORSE FLOAT – WEBB DOCK. NIGHT.

Loud male laughter emanates from in and around Sean's horse float. A group of blokes are sharing a joint. Sean, Brendan, the feral, Podge and Chopper. Brendan is in full flight.

BRENDAN: No, no. It's true. I swear. Judges, company directors, rich pricks. One of the chicks from the sex workers told me. Said the richer and more powerful they were, the more they'd want the living crap whipped out of them. Reckoned it was to atone for making everyone else's life a misery ...

SEAN: And that's your empirical evidence for reckoning half the Cabinet's into bondage?

BRENDAN: Mate, it's written all over them. Look at Reith – the way his beady little eyes blink. Tie me up, whip me 'til I bleed. Make me paaay ... Oooh, that's good ...

Laughter. Chopper and Podge engage the feral in conversation in the background, and Sean leans in to Brendan.

SEAN: You're full of shit, Tully.

BRENDAN: Yeah, well ... What? You were going to entertain this mob with readings from Trotsky?

Sean can't help but envy Brendan's natural skill with people – he makes it look so easy.

SCENE 45. EXT. MAIN GATE – WEBB DOCK. DAY.

Friday, April 17th, 1998. Sean is using his loud hailer. He is saying something along the lines of: Okay. They're coming through. You know what to do.

The 'scab' bus draws close, the driver clearly anticipating the usual noisy obscenities. But this time every single person in the considerable crowd simply turns their back on the bus and remains totally silent. Men, women, unionists, students, greenies, members of the public. Several little old ladies wearing 'WEBB PATRICK DOCK PEACEFUL ASSEMBLY' T-shirts.

It is an eerily powerful moment: hundreds of people, showing their backs to the bus in contempt. Complete silence. The bus moves through, slowly, the driver almost more unnerved by the silence than by the usual rabble.

Sean is at the centre of this, the orchestrator of it. The moment is attenuated. Sean breathes slowly, waiting for someone to break ranks. But no one does.

Inside the bus, some of the 'scabs' have their heads down, hiding their faces. Some wear balaclavas. The expressions of others vary from stubborn defiance to unease, to downright fear.

The bus moves through, goes past the gates. The gates are locked. Sean releases his breath.

And when he looks up he sees, watching him, Janine, her mother Maureen, and his son, Alex. Maureen wears a 'WEBB PATRICK DOCK PEACEFUL ASSEMBLYT' shirt. Janine is in her uniform.

Sean's not sure how to react at first – but the choice is taken from him by Alex bounding over and launching himself into the air for his father to catch. They hug tightly.

SEAN: Hey. Show us that mouth. You've lost a tooth.

ALEX: Yeah. And I got two dollars.

SEAN: Two dollars? Mate, that's more than I got for a whole bloody mouthful …

Maureen and Janine notice the process server approaching.

PROCESS SERVER: Don't suppose you could tell me where Sean McSwain is?

MAUREEN: Yeah. (*Pointing in the opposite direction*) He went that way. Nuggety bloke. Black hair.

PROCESS SERVER: Figures. He's already been a blond and a redhead.

SCENE 46. EXT. MAIN GATE – WEBB DOCK. DAY.

Janine and Sean are walking together. Various assembled protestors wave to or greet Sean as he passes: he is, by now, a well-known figure.

SEAN: You've changed your hair.

JANINE: So've you.

His hair is, of course, a mess. He has hardly had the opportunity for titivation in recent weeks.

SEAN: I'm going for the Che Guevara look.

JANINE: Actually, I'm here for the Nurses' Federation. The committee want to support you guys. I said I'd find out what you need.

SEAN: Bodies. We've got a phone tree. We put it in action when we think we need numbers. Took forever to put it together, but it works. The rule is, nothing gets off the docks. No trucks in. None out.

JANINE: Well organised.

SEAN: What did you expect?

Janine is studying him quizzically.

JANINE: Never thought I'd see you in this position. You seem to've taken to it.

SEAN: I wake up sweating practically every night. Always the same – a truck's got through. Someone's got a container out. You know ...

They walk in silence for some moments.

JANINE: Sean, is there somewhere we can talk?

SEAN: We're talking now.

JANINE: Where are you staying?

SEAN: Bermagui Belle's.

JANINE: What?

SEAN: It's a horse float. It's not much. But it's mine.

SCENE 47. INT./EXT. THE BEER GARDEN – A PUB. DAY.

Sean and Janine have a beer each.

JANINE: We were too young.

SEAN: That's bullshit.

JANINE: You were so serious. About your politics. About everything.

SEAN: When you start work on the waterfront at sixteen, you either get politicised or you die.

JANINE: Think about it, Sean. Night courses in politics. Marxist studies. Industrial law. I wanted to go to Fiji for our honeymoon. But you had to go to Moscow. In winter. For your honeymoon.

SEAN: You said you liked Russia.

JANINE: I said I thought Gorby was cute. It's not the same thing.

SEAN: How could I forget?

There's a story here – but they're not going into it. Not yet.

JANINE: Sean, I didn't want to shoulder the working man's burden at twenty-one. I wanted a boyfriend who'd talk to my friends. I wanted to do all that shit you do ... go dancing, take drugs. And all you wanted to do was sit in your room reading Marx.

SEAN: You know why I stood for this job? To get all the shit out of my head and into my mouth. To force myself to stop being some kind of social bloody retard.

JANINE: To prove something to me?

Sean lets this one go through to the keeper.

SEAN: And now you're here representing the Nurses' Federation. How does that work?

JANINE: I'm grown up now. I've worked out what's important. Though it's getting pretty hard to work out how to be on the left these days. Not as simple as it used to be.

Sean is confused.

SEAN: I dunno what you're saying, Neen.

JANINE: Neither do I.

A pause.

Alex misses you.

Silence for a moment, then she smiles.

I hate to say this, but the Che thing just isn't happening. You need a haircut.

SCENE 48. EXT. MAIN GATE – WEBB DOCK. DAY.

The docks are quieter. Numbers are down a bit. Protestors sit and stand about in weary knots.

Brendan is craning his neck in an attempt to see through to the docks. Tony arrives below him.

BRENDAN: Look at that dickhead in my crane. It's taken him the best part of an hour to lift one fuckin' box. And they reckon this is productivity? If I'd worked that slow, I'd be booted out and told never to show my dial again. Corrigan's bloody managers couldn't manage a pig to get dirty.

TONY: Where's Mac?

BRENDAN: Dunno, why?

TONY: I just drove in past the Coode Road gates. There's less than a handful of us there, and there's cops hanging round. Just got a smell about it.

SCENE 49. INT./EXT. THE BEER GARDEN – THE PUB. DAY.

Sean is sitting in a chair. Janine is behind him, cutting his hair with nail scissors from her handbag. They are alone in the beer garden.

JANINE: That silent thing. With the scabs. Was that your idea?

SEAN: Yeh.

JANINE: It was good.

A silence. Snip snip snip. A sense of growing intimacy, although neither really knows where it is heading.

SEAN: Hey, d'you remember that matriushka doll we bought in that street? The Arbat? With Gorby on the outside?

JANINE: And all the other murderers inside?

SEAN: Have you still got that?

JANINE: Oh, God. I dunno. Somewhere ... Gave it to Mum, I think.

SEAN: Poor old Gorby. Gone down in history as the man who signed the Communist Party out of existence. How does he live with himself, d'you reckon? How does he look in the mirror every day, knowing he signed its death warrant?

Another silence. The comb in his hair, her hand smoothing it, the scissors snipping, her fingers wiping the hair from the back of his neck.

I fuckin' hate this, Neen. I fuckin' hate it.

He reaches up and clutches her hand. She does not move away. He raises the hand and places it on her cheek.

JANINE: Don't, Sean. Don't.

SEAN: Please ...

In any case, he's not going to take 'No' for an answer – and both know she's not going to say it. He takes her face in his hands, kisses and embraces her with the authority of someone who's been doing it, unquestioned, for years.

Then he's moving her away from the table, up against the wall. Kissing her with passion and real intent.

Janine McSwain (Justine Clarke) and Sean McSwain (Anthony Hayes).

JANINE: Sean … we can't … not here …
SEAN: I don't care …
JANINE: Got to go somewhere … where can we go … ?

SCENE 50. EXT. REAR GATE – WEBB DOCK. DAY.

Tony is walking to the smaller, rear gates of the dock. As he walks he sees:

Several policemen rounding up about ten protestors while another cop swings open the big gates and talks into a walkie-talkie.

Some distance away, a truck moves towards the gates. Tony pauses long enough to pick up a lump of cement and then begins to run. He's out of condition and can't move too fast.

He puffs and pants and grimaces. He gets closer, ducking and weaving around the cops.

TONY: Fuckin' played for the Magpies reserves, you pricks …

Finally he reaches the gate moments before the truck does and stands, arms stretched out, in the open gateway. Gasping for breath.

A couple of policemen move in to shift him. The truck moves close and stops.

SERGEANT 1: Keep coming. He'll move.
TONY: You cross here, you're crossing a picket line. You're a scab.

The small group of rounded-up protestors begins to chant: 'Scab, scab, scab!'

The truck is getting closer. Its huge grille is now only metres, and then feet, from Tony's face. The policeman moves in to Tony.

SERGEANT 1: I don't want to do this, mate. But I will pick you up bodily and move you. And if you resist there's a serious risk you'll be hurt.

Tony: the huge grille of the truck; the lump of cement in his hand; the face of the cop; an awareness that other cops are moving closer to him …

Cut to Brendan coming at a sprint. Moving very fast, but not fast enough. He watches as:

Tony drops the lump of cement at his feet, spits on the ground, and walks away. The chanting slows, and fades away: their man has lost his nerve.

And Tony looks up to see that his son has witnessed the whole thing.

SCENE 51. INT. A CHEAP HOTEL ROOM – THE PUB. DAY.

A very basic room upstairs at the pub. Sean's mobile phone, switched off, is discarded on a side table.

Sean watches from the bed as Janine pulls her clothes on. On her lower back, just above her buttocks, is a tattoo. Sean leans across and kisses it.

SEAN: You don't have to go straight away, do you?

JANINE: I'm on night duty. Mum's with the kids.

SEAN: Will you bring Alex to see me again?

Janine hesitates, then plonks herself back on the bed and reaches out to touch his face.

JANINE: I haven't done a very good job of leaving you, have I?

SEAN: Better one than I've done of leaving you.

They're touching each other, necks, shoulders, chests.

JANINE: I've been thinking about – if I touched you, whether I'd still feel ... what I'd feel ...

SEAN: And?

JANINE: I don't know.

SEAN: Do you think you could ever feel it?

JANINE: I ...

SEAN: When? How long 'til you could?

JANINE: I don't know, Sean. Don't ask me. You're like a kid. 'Are we there yet?'

SEAN: Oh, I'm there. I've always been there. The question is, are you?

An abrupt cut to:

SCENE 52. EXT. WEBB DOCK. DAY.

Sean, sprinting along the dock, listening to his mobile phone. He runs straight into Brendan, who grabs him, spinning him around.

BRENDAN: Where the fuck were you? A truck got through at Coode Road.

SEAN: Shit ...

BRENDAN: The old man tried to stop 'em. There was nobody there.

SEAN: Oh, shit. Shit shit shit shit shit ...

He moves away and paces, speed dialling a number on his mobile.

Dave. Sean Mac, mate. Listen, we're down people at Coode Road. Can you get the phone tree happening? As many as you can, pronto. Yeah, yeah. Thanks, mate ...

He rings off and sees Brendan still staring at him.

What are you staring at? I'm not fucking Astro Boy.

BRENDAN: You keep talking about this like it's a war.

SEAN: Isn't it?

BRENDAN: Well, if it was, mate, you'd've just lost your whole platoon. How does it feel, uh?

SCENE 53. EXT. MAIN GATE – WEBB DOCK. DAY.

Sean approaches Tony.

SEAN: Hey. Big fella.

TONY: I chucked a rock. Smashed his windscreen. Didn't kill the prick, worse luck. Still ... you'd better suspend me, union man. Using violence and all. 'Cos these days we'd rather suck 'em off than break their legs, wouldn't we?

SEAN: What are you ... ?

TONY: Come on, then. What's the matter with you? Aren't you going to suspend me?

SEAN: No.

Tony spits on the ground at Sean's feet and stalks off.

SCENE 54. EXT. WEBB DOCK. DAY.

Sean finds Brendan and Cherie unpacking several large boxes of chocolates and lollies, tossing them around to eager protestors.

SEAN: Where did these come from?

BRENDAN: Fell off the back of a truck, mate.

CHERIE: Courtesy of the Manufacturing Workers' Union.

Sean draws Brendan aside.

SEAN: What's going on with your old man? Does he want a medal for chucking a rock, or what?

Brendan doesn't reply.

What?

BRENDAN: You don't get it, do you?

SEAN: Get ... what?

BRENDAN: Mate, why do you think the truck got through?

Sean is puzzled.

'Cos the old man squibbed it. He let the cops move him aside without a peep. Lost his nerve and squibbed it. And his son saw the whole thing.

SEAN: Bren, it doesn't matter. It's my fault anyway ...

BRENDAN: Yeah. It's your fuckin' fault. But it matters.

Silence for a moment.

He always said 'Watch the big talkers. It's always the big talkers that go to water when the heat's on. 'S the quiet ones come through'. Poor old bastard. Failed his own test.

SCENE 55. EXT. MAIN GATE – WEBB DOCK. EVENING.

Tony continues to regale anyone who'll listen. Very little of his dialogue is audible, but it's clear he is loud-mouthedly pushing the blame outwards, away from himself.

TONY: Fuckin' union's lost the plot. Bloody Tas Bull wouldn't've stood for this. Jim Healy. Scabs doing our jobs ...

Sean watches from a distance, eyes filled with compassion.

SCENE 55. INT. FEDERAL COURT – MELBOURNE. DAY.

Burnside is in the zone, summing up his case.

BURNSIDE: During the third week of September last year, in strictest secrecy, Patrick Corporation did three things: it bought back a large number of shares from the four labour-hire companies; and it had each of these four companies sell both their businesses and their assets – all of their assets – to another company within the Patrick group. Thus the companies were stripped to the point of insolvency – an insolvency that came to pass, conveniently, with precision timing, on the evening of April seventh this year when, as we know, the workforce was forcibly ejected from the docks. Thus, ultra conveniently, allowing those companies to argue that they cannot continue operating – and paying their workforce – because they are insolvent. The workers, without consultation in any of this process, would be made redundant and their entitlements paid out by a handy little gift of one hundred and fifty-two million dollars provided, with quite remarkable generosity, if I may say so, by the Federal Government.

Josh is riveted by Burnside's every word.

SCENE 56. EXT. WEBB DOCK. EVENING.

It is cooling down, moving on towards evening.

Sean sits on the edge of his horse float feeling pretty lousy. Tiredly running through the union's roster.

Voices from nearby penetrate his consciousness.

CHERIE: I haven't seen him all day ...

PROCESS SERVER: Right.

He chucks his files, his legal envelopes and his briefcase on the ground. He is having a full-on meltdown.

That is it. I've spent days chasing round these docks. Sent on wild goose chases. Mocked and ridiculed by the good people of the labour movement. I'm not an agent of Satan. I've got kids. I'm in debt until I'm eighty-two and four fifths, and that's assuming a maintenance of current interest rates. I'm a wage slave just like you are. You're not the only noble victims here. What you are is a bunch of overweight, overpaid, self-centred, bludging bloody ... bloody narcissists.

Sean steps forward.

SEAN: I think you're looking for me. I'm Sean McSwain.

The process server, sheepish after his immoderate display of temper, bends down, scrabbles on the ground for his legal documents. Sean waits.

PROCESS SERVER: Sean McSwain. It's my duty to serve on you this Supreme Court order, injuncting you not to attend any protest at any dock in the country. If you persist in ignoring this order, you will be held in contempt of court.

SEAN: I understand. Can I just ask ...

He gestures at the particularly rough-headed group of wharfies that have assembled to watch the fun. Podge, Chopper, Nuts. And several more.

... Do these blokes look like a bunch of narcissists to you?

The process server shrugs apologetically.

PROCESS SERVER: I've been doing a night course in psychology.

SCENE 57. INT. FEDERAL COURT – MELBOURNE. EVENING.

NORTH: I suspect it may take longer to reach a conclusion here than we might have anticipated ...

In the gallery, Combet swears under his breath

COMBET: Fuck ...

BURNSIDE: Your Honour, counsel would be prepared to attend the court over the weekend, if that would be of assistance. I submit that the longer the situation on the docks is allowed to continue, the more the status quo would become entrenched, and the more difficult it will be to reverse.

NORTH: Mr Burnside, I'm well aware of the urgency and public interest in the issues surrounding this case. It's regrettable that I'm not in a position to hand down a decision immediately. However, what you are asking me to do is to contravene the Corporations Act and order an administrator to continue operating an unprofitable business. I will give careful attention to all the arguments over the weekend and if necessary beyond. The court is adjourned.

Josh lowers his head in exhaustion. Burnside, as ever, maintains his calm demeanour. In the gallery, a deeply anxious Combet reaches for his mobile phone to call Coombs.

SCENE 58. INT. WAITING AREA – ABC RADIO. EVENING.

Sydney. John Coombs is sitting, waiting to appear on the ABC's PM programme. He is listening on his mobile, his responses unusually guarded.

COOMBS: Yes. Yep. Okay. Got that. See you.

The reason for his restraint is sitting next to him, clearly hearing the same news on his mobile: Chris Corrigan.

CORRIGAN: Yep. Thank you.

It is almost comic as both men pocket their mobiles at exactly the same instant and stare anywhere in the room except at each other.

Meanwhile the PM broadcast plays on overhead speakers.

ABC RADIO JOURNALIST: (*voice over*) Well, it's going to be a long, nail-biting weekend for both parties. The union needs the pickets to stay put for moral sway with the public, and, naturally, as a fallback strategy if it fails in court. Corrigan, on the other hand, needs to prove to his bankers and his shareholders that he can keep his business operating ... and that means getting those pickets shifted and the cargo moving through. With public opinion increasingly swinging in behind the union ...

An assistant comes in from the studio and invites Coombs to come with her. Coombs rises stiffly and follows. Corrigan watches him go.

SCENE 59. INT. THE LIVING ROOM – COOMBS' HOUSE. NIGHT.

John Coombs unlocks the front door, swings it open and comes into the house. He closes the door behind him, leans on it for a moment to rest his tired eyes. He's exhausted. Gwen appears from the kitchen with a steaming cup of tea in her hand. They embrace, and he takes the tea.

COOMBS: How was your day, love?

GWEN: Oh, Jenny and I played games with the ASIO phone tap. Guess where you were this time?

COOMBS: Where?

GWEN: On a top-secret trip to China to borrow money from the Communist party.

Coombs manages a smile ... just. Gwen glances at him with concern. Is he going to make it through this?

SCENE 60. EXT. WEBB DOCK. NIGHT.

The chill of the evening has descended. Forty-four gallon drums are alight. A small group of rather earnest musicians is strumming acoustic guitars and singing Billy-Bragg-type pro-union songs. A number of protestors, rugged up against the cold, sit around joining in. The flags of the various supportive unions, the CFMEU, ETU, MWU, PSU and so on float in a light sea breeze. The atmosphere is almost celebratory.

Sean is sitting, as usual, on the lip of his horse float. He is on his mobile phone, hearing the news that the court case has been adjourned. He could practically weep.

SEAN: ... Afraid that might happen. Yep. Okay, mate.

He rings off.

Very slowly, Tony Tully walks over to him. Sits down. And hands Sean a paper plate.

TONY: Bloke with the bubblegum in his hair said you liked these. Reckon they look like stewed turds myself.

Lentil burgers.

SEAN: Hey, d'you reckon this mob knows anything by Bon Jovi?

TONY: Anything'd be better than this God-awful bloody wailing.

SEAN: You reckon that's why capitalism won, uh? Better music?

TONY: Nah. Just that people suck. Hey, did you see Podge doing golf practice down along the fence line? Reckons he got two birdies, an eagle, and a hole in one. Smacked that miserable one-armed foreman right in the solar plexus.

A silence.

What happened with the wankers in the wigs?

SEAN: Adjourned 'til Monday.

TONY: We're not going to get back in, are we?

SEAN: I dunno, mate.

TONY: Coombs is cutting our balls off; you know that, don't you? When did the old Waterside Workers' Federation rely on a bunch of lawyers to fight their battles? The law's not going to come out on our side – the law props up the bloody system. We're losin' who we are. This new fuckin' corporate, business-friendly image. Makes me want to puke. You put a DJ's suit on a garbo, he's still a fuckin' garbo, isn't he? And we're just sitting here on our hands, letting 'em screw us. Give me a fight, I'll have it. Let me break their kneecaps. But this … this is just rotting my intestines …

SEAN: Mate, Corrigan's the enemy. Not John Coombs.

TONY: Yeah?

SEAN: I'm sorry about the truck. All right?

TONY: I voted for you.

He gets stiffly to his feet and walks off, no longer the stubborn pugilist.

SEAN: I'll do better.

He stands, almost as though to follow Tony.

I'll do better, mate …

TONY: Too bloody late. If Corrigan offers me the handshake, I'll take it. Not hanging round in a job with no heart and a union with no soul.

He mooches off. Sean has no time to be too shattered. His mobile phone is ringing.

SEAN: Sean McSwain. Yep?

His face, if its possible, looks even more worried.

SCENE 61. INT. THE HALLWAY AND LIVING ROOM – COMBET'S HOUSE. NIGHT.

Combet walks into the house, exhausted. From the living room he hears a noisy game of Five Hundred in progress. He leans on the hall wall for a moment, and closes his eyes, not really feeling up to company. Then he pushes himself forward and forces a smile as he moves into the living room and sees Petra with three friends around the table. General greetings: 'Greg', 'Hi', 'How's it going?', 'Hello, stranger'.

COMBET: G'day.

And with that his mobile phone rings. Greg shrugs – no rest for the wicked.

Hello …

The bidding in the game continues – 'Seven hearts', 'Eight no trumps' – as Greg absorbs a particular piece of news.

… Uh huh. You think this is the one? … Yep. See you.

He rejoins the group.

Um. Apparently they've cancelled all police leave for the weekend. Source says they might be planning a move on the docks.

To his surprise the group around the table stands, begins to shoulder swags and backpacks.

SUSAN: Well, we're all boy scouts here. We're ready for 'em. Waste not, want not …

She lifts a plate of biscuits and shoves them into her pack.

COMBET: Thanks, everybody. I ...

PETRA: I'm coming with you.

COMBET: We can't take the kids ...

PETRA: Clara's old enough to mind the young ones. I'm coming. (*To the group*) It's a conspiracy, you know. I was going to win slam-no-trumps for sure.

Greg opens his mouth to say 'Thank you', but Petra raises a hand.

Don't say it.

The rest of the group moves outside as she goes into the kitchen, flicks a few switches, rapidly fills a couple of plastic bottles of water.

I should have known: I've got a roast in the oven. These days I think, 'Well, Petra ... pop a roast on. You'll end up down the docks for sure. And at least you'll see Greg. Maybe even in the flesh and not on TV'. That's what I do. Did you know that? Sit up every night watching *Lateline* to catch a glimpse of my life partner.

Flick. Click. Gush. Thump.

COMBET: Is that it?

PETRA: No. I've got my period. So don't say 'Thank you'. I don't want to hear it.

As he watches her ultra-efficient organisation, Greg finds the beginnings of tears in his eyes.

COMBET: (*sotto voce*) I was going to say, 'I love you'. Is that acceptable?

SCENE 62. EXT. MAIN GATE – WEBB DOCK. NIGHT.

Friday, April 17th, 1998. Sean is on the mobile.

SEAN: We – um – we're not abandoning the protest, but I'll do my best ... No violence ... Yeah. Uh, Sergeant ... how many? We heard four ... ? Seven hundred ... Yeah ... Yep. Okay.

He winds the call up quickly and moves rapidly to where he has a bucket stored under the horse float. He vomits into it. Finishes, leans back, wiping his mouth.

To see Brendan watching.

BRENDAN: Stage fright, mate?

Sean nods.

SCENE 63. INT. JANINE'S BEDROOM. NIGHT.

Janine is reading a magazine in a pool of light. She picks up her ringing mobile phone.

JANINE: Hello? Yeah, I'm the Nurses' Federation rep. What ... ?

SCENE 64. EXT. WEBB DOCK. NIGHT.

A bucket of water is tipped onto the fire in a 44 gallon drum. A second fire is doused. Plumes of black smoke spiral into the sky. Embers waft onto the breeze.

Helicopters can be heard overhead.

The docks' landscape looks like something from Mad Max: railway tracks have been welded into weird shapes, there are blocks of concrete and steel and an overturned semi-trailer.

The Victorian Trades Hall Choir sings a rallying version of 'The Internationale'.

More cars arrive. More and more people join the group. (In reality it was, by now, about three thousand strong.)

People move into formation – arms linked, hands clutching the belts of those in front.

Combet and Petra move in to take their places in the front line. Bill Kelty is there. Sean. Tony and Lyn. Brendan and Cherie.

SCENE 65. EXT. MAIN GATE – WEBB DOCK. NIGHT.

Josh and Tali have just arrived and are making their way from the rear through the group of demonstrators.

TALI: John Coombs'll skin you for this.

JOSH: My old man's here somewhere. My sister. My Nan, for fuck's sake. I am not missing this.

But moving through more quickly, now, is Janine, pushing her way towards the front of the throng. Until, finally, she's near to Sean, who turns and sees her. A combination of longing and uncertainty in his face – how does she feel about him? Is there a chance?

He loosens his grip on the arm of the old woman beside him to allow Janine in. Janine locks herself in to the line.

SEAN: Thanks for coming down.

JANINE: Thank the Nurses' Federation. I was in bed with *Who* magazine.

Shouts from behind them. Groans. 'They've stopped again.' The crowd remains with arms linked but relaxes. This standoff is going on and on.

CHERIE: Jeez, I wish they'd get on with it. I'm freezing my bloody tits off out here.

The voice of an ABC reporter cranks up loudly over the union's public address system. She is broadcasting live on her mobile phone. Little by little the crowd falls silent. And, as the reporter's voice takes over, there is a slow ...

FEMALE ABC REPORTER: ... It's been a stand-off down here at Webb Dock for several hours now. The police move forward, the crowd begins to chant, the police stop. The police helicopter is still hovering overhead, and it won't be too long before the day begins to break. A significant number of the police are not wearing badges, a precaution in case anyone is injured if there's a tussle ...

... Fade to black.

SCENE 66. INT. LIMBO. DAY.

Cherie Snape addresses the camera.

CHERIE: Bren says it's my own fault for getting around dressed in a hanky. But I had a chill right through to my kidneys. It went on for hours. The cops came forward, we'd get ready, they'd move back. Forward, back, forward, forward, back, back. It was like doing a line dance on Mars. The one consolation – and Bren's spewing about this one – was I got to hold Greg Combet's hand. For five hours. He is hot.

SCENE 67. EXT. MAIN GATE – WEBB DOCK. NIGHT.

Sean lifts his loudhailer.

SEAN: Everyone. Please stay in formation. Passive resistance. No violence. And remain linked to the person beside you and in front of you. The workers … united … will never be defeated.

The chant takes hold. And seems to roll in waves through the crowd. The workers, united, will never be defeated …

The police begin to inch forward. Little by little. The tension bristles again. They stare each other down.

Sean and Janine are in the crowd.

You're shaking.

JANINE: I'm cold.

SEAN: Neen … ?

JANINE: Don't say it, Sean. Don't ask me if I'm there yet …

SCENE 68. INT. LIMBO. DAY.

Josh Bornstein addresses the camera.

JOSH: You could see the whites of their eyes. And all the clichés start rushing up to meet you. All the footage of riot shields and bloodshed. And I kind of wished Tali wasn't beside me, if it got ugly. And then I heard someone say – I think it was Combet … 'Fuck me dead, it's the cavalry'. And marching up behind the cops were hundreds of CFMEU blokes. So there's us. The cops. The CFMEU. A perfect pincer tactic.

SCENE 69. EXT. MAIN GATE – WEBB DOCK. NIGHT.

Another group of unionists carrying CFMEU flags are marching up behind the police, trapping them in a pincer movement. The police are caught between the MUA-led crowd on one side and the CFMEU on the other.

Some faces amongst the police register flickers of fear and anxiety. This is potentially a very ugly situation. The CFMEU members begin to shout abuse at the police. Some spit at them. Combet, Sean, Kelty and others start to look worried.

Sean breaks from formation and moves to the police commander.

SERGEANT 1: Pull these blokes off, or there'll be a shit-fight.

He means the CFMEU. Who are looking very, very aggressive.

Sean moves rapidly through the police formation with a couple of Trades Hall representatives to stand between the police and the CFMEU. Sean raises his loudhailer. He is very nervous.

SEAN: We owe you blokes a beer, for this. And I think we can safely say it's all over. Our friends in uniform here are going to move quietly out and we're going to call it a night. We don't want any violence, fellas. We've won this one without it. Let's keep it tidy.

SCENE 70. INT. LIMBO. DAY.

Sean McSwain addresses the camera.

SEAN: You don't think. You just breathe. They say your parasympathetic nervous system's engaged. Fight or flight. I did this self-hypnosis thing once, years ago. And it came back, and I'm standing there, trying to talk these CFMEU blokes down, trying to get the cops out, clear, and I'm just saying to myself: 'Floating ... floating ... floating ...' You don't think. You just do it.

SCENE 71. EXT. MAIN GATE – WEBB DOCK. NIGHT.

It is very, very tense, and Sean is holding his breath as he more or less ushers the police through the unionists' ranks. But the unionists do as bid. There is no violence, and, as the last police move through and away, there's a spontaneous cheer and a huge burst of applause from the unionist throng.

Suddenly, there's chaos. Shouting and hugging and dancing. Sean is spinning round, trying to find Janine in the crowd. And then, without warning, he is hoisted onto the shoulders of several hefty unionists – a minor hero of the day.

He's up there, embarrassed, asking to be put down, eyes scanning the crowd for Janine.

Brendan and Cherie shake his legs as though shaking hands.

BRENDAN: Hey, Mac. Good on you, mate ...

SEAN: Piss off, will ya?

But he's smiling. Very embarrassed. And now, finally, he sees Janine. She's looking up at him, signalling that she's going home. Sean's face: is she there yet? But he can't get to her to ask, and now she's moving away through the crowd, leaving the question unanswered ...

SCENE 72. EXT. MAIN GATE – WEBB DOCK. DAWN.

Saturday, April 18th, 1998. A bleak and chilly dawn. The fuss is over. Almost all of the earlier throng have left. Sean is sitting around a burning 44 gallon drum, with Chopper, Podge, Nuts and the feral.

FERAL: You guys need lessons in passive resistance. You don't need these kind of numbers. You just need smarter tactics.

PODGE: Yeah. So what'd you do down on the fuckin' Franklin? Poison 'em with fuckin' lentil burgers?

FERAL: You've got the car on the road, right? You oxytorch a ringbolt to the other side of the chassis. Then you handcuff yourself to the ringbolt. They can't move the car without pulling your arm off. Never fails.

PODGE: Uuuh. Shit.

Some distance away, a police car pulls up.

SEAN: Oh, shit. Here it comes ...

A single police sergeant is walking towards them – the same sergeant Sean dealt with earlier. The little group falls silent as the sergeant approaches. Finally, Sean stands to meet him.

If you're here to haul me off for contempt of court, just take me somewhere warm ...

SERGEANT 1: Haul you off? Jeez, we'd have a pretty full lockup. That stupid bastard judge has injuncted half the bloody country. Came to say you did good tonight. My blokes don't want to be here any more than you lot do, you know that. Could'a' been very ugly, and you made sure it wasn't.

Sean is so stunned he can barely speak. Then he notices that the Sergeant has an oddly shaped manila envelope in his hand.

Someone turned this in at the station. Must've got dropped in all the fuss.

Sean takes it, still silent.

Early opener at Williamstown. We're going for a beer. You're welcome to join us.

He turns and goes back to the car.

FERAL: That never happened on the Franklin.

Sean opens the envelope: from it slides a Russian matriushka doll, about six inches high. The figure it represents is Mikhail Gorbachev, birthmark and all.

SCENE 73. EXT. WEBB DOCK. DAWN.

Sean walks slowly through the debris littered landscape of the docks. The sun is just beginning to light up the sky. It looks like a war zone. He is burning with all kinds of emotions – pride, weariness, fear, hope.

SCENE 74. INT./EXT. SEAN'S HORSE FLOAT – WEBB DOCK. DAWN.

He climbs into his horse float, sits down. And only then does he twist the little matriushka doll, separating it into two halves. Inside is a folded Polaroid photograph of Sean and Janine some years ago. Both have their hair slicked back and down to make it invisible. Both wear red CCCP T-shirts. And both have large, brown birthmarks, shaped just like Gorby's, across their foreheads, probably drawn with eye makeup. They grin stupidly at the camera.

Sean begins to cry. Eyes watering, throat choking. And then come wrenching sobs, as though all the pent up fear and loss and hope is being released in one horrible, painful moment.

He cries for a long time and then, slowly, fades to black.

END OF PART THREE

SCENE 1. INT. THE LAUNDRY VAN. DAY.

The laundry van is driving towards the docks at Port Botany. It is old and the shock absorbers are shot to pieces. Frank is driving.

FRANK: You all right back there?

Corrigan is in the back, his long legs cramped up around his chest, being bumped around on the hard metal surface.

CORRIGAN: Believe me, Frank, this is how I always spend my Sundays.

SCENE 2. INT./EXT. THE LAUNDRY VAN – PATRICK PORT BOTANY DOCK. DAY.

Sunday April 19th, 1998. The laundry van inches along the docks. Corrigan peeps out, and sees:

The crowd.

People having barbecues. A few people having a sing-along.

And, up ahead, a raised platform from which John Coombs is addressing the crowd.

COOMBS: Chris Corrigan's trouble is he doesn't understand the history of the waterfront. You take on one of us, you take on all. Men, women and children of the labour movement: one … more … day. One more day 'til the Federal Court reinstates us. One more day 'til we send Chris Corrigan packing to the dunce's corner to learn a history lesson he'll never forget …

Coombs has the crowd in the palm of his hand. He climbs down from the platform, to be greeted with applause and backslapping. Corrigan notices, in particular, Coombs' son, Garry, reaching up from his wheelchair to shake his father's hand.

He keeps watching as two elderly ladies, wearing MUA T-shirts,

Chris's war: Chris Corrigan (Geoff Morrell) waits to go on air.

embrace and kiss Coombs and hand him a cake they've made for him.

CORRIGAN: Okay, Frank. That'll do. Take me back to jail.

BASTARD BOYS

PART FOUR: CHRIS'S WAR

SCENE 3. EXT. FEDERAL COURT – MELBOURNE. DAY.

Tuesday, April 21st, 1998. There's a big crowd outside the court. Lots of media, lots of cameras. The air is filled with anticipation.

SCENE 4. INT. FEDERAL COURT – MELBOURNE. DAY.

The court is packed to the rafters. Everyone is holding their breath. Josh Bornstein sits with his back to Justice North, facing Burnside and the rest of his legal team.

NORTH: ... By dividing the companies into those which employed the workers and those which owned the capital, the Patrick group put in place a structure which made it easier to dismiss the entire workforce. It is arguable on the evidence that this was done because the employees were members of the union.

Josh begins to feel the tears prickling the back of his eyes. In the gallery, Combet finally allows himself to breathe.

There is an arguable case that Patrick has breached the contracts of employment and engaged in an unlawful conspiracy. I therefore find that Patrick should reinstate its workers as soon as possible.

And the tears are running down Josh's cheeks.

The Patrick barrister, Middleton, is already reaching for his mobile phone. Reporters rush to file their stories.

SCENE 5. INT. PATRICK HEAD OFFICE. DAY.

Everything stops amongst the assembled group of Patrick department heads as Corrigan's mobile phone, waiting in the centre of the table, rings. Rings again.

Finally, Corrigan answers it.

CORRIGAN: Chris Corrigan.

He listens.

Appeal it.

SCENE 6. INT. A CORRIDOR – FEDERAL COURT. DAY.

Greg Combet, trying not to bubble over with excitement, talks on his mobile.

COMBET: He's going to appeal. We're not out of the woods ... John, stay on message, will you? ...

SCENE 7. INT. THE BOARDROOM – MUA. DAY.

Cameras and microphones are focussed on John Coombs as he paces around the boardroom, listening to his mobile. He is breathing deeply, the smile creeping onto his face.

COOMBS: Right you are, brother ...

He ends the call, puts the phone aside, and faces the media.

This is an immense victory. This victory assures the Maritime Union, as if we were in any doubt, that we have the moral high ground. I have guaranteed Justice North that we can have those men back at work within the hour ... and that they'll work for nothing for two weeks until the Patrick Labour companies are solvent again. Can't be fairer than that, can I?

An immense grin swamps his weary face.

SCENE 8. INT. THE MEDIA ROOM – PATRICK HEAD OFFICE. EVENING.

Corrigan, by contrast, is not smiling as he faces a rabble of reporters, microphones and cameras. A series of questions are hurled at him. 'How do you feel?' 'Will you appeal?' 'How's your share price?' 'Will you comply with the order?'

CORRIGAN: The order is unworkable. I will now be forced to pay two workforces when I can barely afford to pay one. Yes, there will no doubt be further pressure on the Patrick share price, and I'd like to reassure our shareholders that we are doing everything we can to ensure their best interests. What's that?

SYDNEY JOURNALIST: How soon can the MUA members return to work?

CORRIGAN: There are, I understand, security issues. My port managers actually fear for their safety with the wharfies, and understandably, given the kind of harassment they've endured so far.

SCENE 9. INT. CORRIGAN'S OFFICE – PATRICK HEAD OFFICE. DAY.

Corrigan strides back into his office to find Jenny, his secretary, holding out the phone.

JENNY: Citibank.

Corrigan rolls his eyes, mouths 'Fuck'. And takes the phone.

He rests the mouthpiece against his chest, and remarks, to anyone who might be listening:

CORRIGAN: Can you believe I used to be a bloody banker? (*Into the phone*) Ken. How are you? No, well, we're not popping the champagne just yet. We did agree to four weeks, though. My reckoning, that gives me another week before you string me up …

SCENE 10. INT. THE CAR PARK – HOTEL. NIGHT.

Corrigan emerges from the fire escape, glances over his shoulder. Nothing. He moves quickly across the underground car park in the direction of his motorbike. Yesss! Made it! He is just saddling up and preparing to don his helmet when Frank the security man comes running breathlessly after him.

FRANK: Mr Corrigan.

'Oh, fuck', thinks Corrigan. He raises his hands – sprung.

CORRIGAN: I'm getting cabin fever, Frank.

FRANK: Mr Corrigan. It's not safe. If you want to go out, I'll be perfectly happy to take you in the –

CORRIGAN *and* FRANK: – Camouflaged vehicle.

And there, in front of them, is the hated laundry van.

SCENE 11. INT. CORRIGAN'S OFFICE – PATRICK HEAD OFFICE. NIGHT.

Corrigan prowls around the office, talking on his mobile phone to Valerie in Italy. Below him is a vista of the city that he cannot access. Nearby is a half-eaten takeaway meal.

CORRIGAN: We're haemorrhaging, Val ... I just ... never expected Coombs to play it this well.

On the muted television Coombs is being interviewed on Lateline. *Corrigan watches the screen as his son comes on the line.*

Hello, Joe. Come sta? I do beg your pardon. Come stai?

His eyes are fixed on John Coombs.

Pull away from Corrigan and move towards the glittering, twinkling, eternal lights of the city, until:

SCENE 12. EXT. MAIN GATE – WEBB DOCK. NIGHT.

Melbourne. Another man on the phone to a distant child. Around him, the lights of the still working dock, and the lingering protesters in clusters. It is cold. As he speaks, he walks towards his horse float.

SEAN: Hey, you should be in bed, little mate. Mum says you've got a trip to the zoo tomorrow. The meerkats? What the ... ? Yeah, go now, quick, before Mum does her 'nana ... Teeth!

Janine comes on the line.

Neen. Tell me something. What the fuck's a meerkat? Buy me a book about them? Yeah, right. So – ahm ... am I going to see you soon?

Now inside the float, he looks up at where he has fixed two photos to the wall: one of his son Alex, and the one he had earlier, of himself and Janine in their CCCP T-shirts.

SCENE 13. INT. THE LOUNGE ROOM – DEREK CORRIGAN'S HOUSE. DAY.

A tall, dark, solid man stands watching the news. On close inspection he bears a faint resemblance to the man on the screen, Chris Corrigan, continuing last night's interview.

CORRIGAN: (*on television*) ... My managers, all over the country, have been harassed, threatened, assaulted and had their families subjected to quite shocking abuse. I'll be forever grateful to them for their loyalty and their courage ...

He's choking up, close to breaking down.

Is that it? Okay. Thanks very much.

Derek freezes the frame on the image and looks at Corrigan's face – the news has clearly been videotaped.

SCENE 14. INT. THE HALL – DEREK CORRIGAN'S HOUSE. DAY.

The man and his wife are rummaging through the phone book.

WENDY: Well, who? Who do we call?

DEREK: I dunno. The union?

WENDY: What are they called? Waterside Workers' Federation ... ?

DEREK: No no no no. 'MUA, here to stay.' Maritime Union. Maritime Union of Australia.

They rummage through the phone book.

WENDY: It's not there

DEREK: It must be. I can't read without my glasses.

He rummages, finds his specs, puts them on.

WENDY: Dial 'Directory'. Oh one three ...

Derek does.

DEREK: The Maritime Union of Australia. Thanks ... Nine two two ...

He and his wife look at each other. Here goes ...

Derek dials the number. Waits. Faintly a voice on the end says, 'Good morning. Maritime Union'.

Um, yes, hello. Is John Coombs available, please? ... Tell him it's the brother of the Devil incarnate.

SCENE 15. EXT. MAIN GATE – WEBB DOCK. DAY.

Coombs is standing in the tray of a utility, addressing the crowd.

COOMBS: 'Despicable'. That's what he said. Out of the mouth of Chris Corrigan's own brother. So there you have it: Corrigan's brother, a unionist!

There's a burst of applause.

Garry sits up straighter in his wheelchair: That's my old man ...

SCENE 16. INT. THE HALL AND LOUNGE ROOM – DEREK CORRIGAN'S HOUSE. DAY.

The phone in Derek's hall is ringing. Derek comes running from the bathroom, wrapped in a towel, dripping.

In the lounge room two photographers and a TV camera crew are waiting for him. He is already under media siege.

DEREK: Be with you blokes in a minute. Sorry to keep you. (*Into the phone*) Hello?

Cross-cut as required with:

SCENE 17. INT. CORRIGAN'S OFFICE – PATRICK HEAD OFFICE. DAY.

CORRIGAN: Derek?

DEREK: Christopher. Didn't know you had my number.

CORRIGAN: John Coombs is down at the docks spouting all kinds of stuff he claims you've said ... Is it true?

DEREK: I called him, yeah.

CORRIGAN: This is none of your business, Derek. You don't know a bloody thing about it.

DEREK: Sorry, Chris. But when you start attacking workers and the conditions of workers, then it is my business ...

CORRIGAN: Listen, if you want your fifteen minutes of fame, don't do it on my back. There's no place for you in any of this. Stay out of it.

Corrigan puts the phone down and strides out past Jenny and his other office workers.

I'm going out.

SCENE 18. INT. RECEPTION – PATRICK HEAD OFFICE. DAY.

Corrigan stalks towards the lift. Frank, the security man, puffs after him.

FRANK: Mr Corrigan –

CORRIGAN: I'm going out, Frank.
FRANK: But –
CORRIGAN: I'm going out.

SCENE 19. INT. THE HALL AND LOUNGE ROOM – DEREK CORRIGAN'S HOUSE. NIGHT.

Derek, exhausted and stressed, walks in.

WENDY: Your father rang. Wants you to call him back.

Derek says nothing, takes the phone, dials.

DEREK: Dad. It's Derek ... I'm not attacking Christopher, Dad. I'm taking issue with his business practices ...

There's a long silence. Derek looks as though he's been kicked in the guts.

You do have a second son, Dad. You've got two sons ...

SCENE 20. INT./EXT. COOMBS' CAR – A CITY STREET. DAY.

Coombs' car is stopped at the lights on the way back into the city from the Sydney docks. Just for a moment he allows his head to drop and lean forward onto his hands on the wheel. He is getting very close to physical and mental exhaustion.

The burble of the car radio can be heard.

ABC RADIO JOURNALIST: Such is the level of public interest in the outcome of this case that, for the first time in history, a Federal Court decision is to be televised live. No fewer than four television networks will interrupt normal scheduling to bring the finding to the nation ...

The driver behind Coombs honks his horn: Get moving!

SCENE 21. INT. PUB NEAR MELBOURNE COURTS. DAY.

Josh Bornstein and Greg Combet in the gloom of a city pub, both drinking water. Combet glances restlessly at his watch. The wait is agonising.

JOSH: This is going to settle.

COMBET: Corrigan won't settle. I know him. He'll fight until every dock in the country's littered with corpses. I know him, Josh.

JOSH: We're going to win. And this is going to settle.

Combet doesn't reply. His head is down. He, too, is close to exhaustion.

COMBET: I haven't seen my daughter in weeks. I've put her through a break-up ... dropped her into a new family ... and now I'm not there.

SCENE 22. INT. FEDERAL COURT – MELBOURNE. DAY.

April 23rd, 1998. A series of step-printed images:

People begin to file in.

More people. And more. The galleries are crammed full. There are members of the union side in the audience: Greg Combet, Sean McSwain. And, unusually, Brendan Tully.

The legal teams walk in. Patrick's team. The union team: Josh, Burnside and the rest.

SCENE 23. EXT. MAIN GATE – PATRICK PORT BOTANY DOCK. DAY.

Sydney. John and Gwen Coombs, Garry, and many others take up positions in front of a television set powered from one of the power poles outside the dock gates.

SCENE 24. EXT. MAIN GATE – WEBB DOCK. DAY.

A similar image in Melbourne: Tony Tully, Lyn, Cherie and numerous others cluster around a television.

SCENE 25. INT. THE LOUNGE ROOM – DEREK CORRIGAN'S HOUSE. DAY.

Derek and Wendy in front of the television.

SCENE 26. INT. CORRIGAN'S OFFICE – PATRICK HEAD OFFICE. DAY.

Corrigan, Paul and his office staff, clustered around the television.

SCENE 27. INT. FEDERAL COURT – MELBOURNE. DAY.

The wait has been agonising. You could cut the atmosphere in the crowded court with a knife. And, suddenly, out of nowhere, Brendan Tully jumps up on the bar table. There is some consternation: this is Not Done. Sean, in particular, looks startled.

BRENDAN: John Howard walks into a doctor's surgery. He's got a frog stuck to his forehead. Not a big one. Just your ordinary, common or garden frog. And the doc – he's a bit surprised, naturally – says, 'Well, sir, what seems to be the problem?' And the frog answers: 'I dunno, mate. I woke up this morning and I had this lump stuck to my arse'.

It brings the house down. Rolls of laughter, waves of laughter, people rocking with laughter, crying with laughter, and this laughter seems to just go on and on, until …

TIPSTAFF: Order, all stand.

Everyone in the courtroom stands as the three Federal Court judges make their way into the court. Lights beam. Cameras roll.

It seems to take an eternity for the judges to settle into their places. And then a second eternity for Justice Wilcox to open his papers, take a deep breath, and begin.

JUSTICE WILCOX: I would like to preface this finding with a statement of what this case is not about. It is not a case about whether or not reform is either necessary or desirable on the Australian waterfront. It is purely about the legality of the current situation. Courts have to rule on the legality of the means, whatever view individual judges may have about the desirability of the end. Further, it is not possible to remain unswayed by the potency of the interests at stake in this case, nor by the media coverage of events. The court, therefore, has brought its analysis and its experience to bear purely on the legal fine print utilised to produce the current situation ...

Perhaps slight slow-motion now, cutting to the principals:

SCENE 28. EXT. MAIN GATE – PATRICK PORT BOTANY DOCK. DAY.

Coombs.

SCENE 29. EXT. MAIN GATE – WEBB DOCK. DAY.

Tony and Lyn.

SCENE 30. INT. FEDERAL COURT – MELBOURNE. DAY.

Combet.

Josh.

Waiting for the verditct. Above: the Coombs family, Gwen (Deborah Kennedy), John (Colin Friels) and Garry (Christopher Widdows). Below: Julian Burnside (Rhys Muldoon).

SCENE 31. INT. THE LOUNGE ROOM – DEREK CORRIGAN'S HOUSE. DAY.

Derek.

SCENE 32. INT. CORRIGAN'S OFFICE – PATRICK HEAD OFFICE. DAY.

And Chris Corrigan.

Waiting. Desperate for Wilcox to come to the point.

SCENE 33. INT. FEDERAL COURT – MELBOURNE. DAY.

JUSTICE WILCOX: We have read and carefully considered the whole of Justice North's reasons for judgement, and we find them free from apellable error.

Combet's head is down. His glasses are off. He presses his fingers into the corners of his eyes to stem the flow of tears.

SCENE 34. EXT. MAIN GATE – PATRICK PORT BOTANY DOCK. DAY.

John Coombs leaps out of his chair with joy. And hugs Gwen firmly. And the two of them begin a little jitterbug amid the cheering throng.

Garry watches his father, aware of his exhaustion, hoping this means the worst is over.

SCENE 35. INT. CORRIGAN'S OFFICE – PATRICK HEAD OFFICE. DAY.

Total silence as Wilcox continues talking. Corrigan does not move.

JUSTICE WILCOX: The court has carefully considered the issues raised by Patrick in relation to the potential of violence on the docks, but our position remains. Vendetta is not the Australian way. All parties will need to exercise restraint in adjusting to the changed arrangements required by Justice North's orders; provided there is proper leadership, we are confident they will …

Finally, after some moments, Corrigan stands and quietly leaves the room.

SCENE 36. INT. THE MEETING ROOM – MAURICE, BLACKBURN, CASHMAN. DAY.

Josh pops the cork of an expensive bottle of champagne and pours it for his team. Tali is with them, equally delighted by the outcome.

Burnside's mobile phone rings.

BURNSIDE: Julian Burnside … Very well.

He hangs up and turns to the team.

You might have to pop a spoon in that, Josh. Ken Hayne's waiting for us at the High Court. They want a stay on the order.

SCENE 37. EXT. JOHN'S HOUSE – NORTHWOOD. NIGHT.

Chris Corrigan, helmet in hand, walks up the path of a comfortable North Shore home. His friend John opens the door.

JOHN: Chris. Come in. The red's open and breathing.

CORRIGAN: I've slipped the leash. Don't tell anyone.

SCENE 38. INT. CHAMBERS – HIGH COURT. NIGHT.

The two legal teams are in chambers with Justice Ken Hayne. Josh is sitting to the side with Tali as Burnside argues their case. Josh is working very hard to keep his anger under control.

HAYNE: Well, Mr Burnside. Your friend here has put something of a hair-raising proposition: without a stay on the order the Patrick managers face the prospect of allowing the MUA back in the gates by lunchtime tomorrow. My colleagues in the Federal Court might have faith that civilised behaviour will prevail. On the basis of past form, I'm afraid I'm not quite so sanguine ...

BURNSIDE: In our submission, Your Honour, even if it is only for symbolic effect, it would be, to say the least, unkind and, at the worst extreme, potentially unsettling at the waterfront if a symbolic victory of this scale were robbed from the union.

HAYNE: Robbed, Mr Burnside? A little hyperbolic, don't you think? And perhaps more than a little premature?

Even the ever-implacable Burnside seems distressed by this tone. Josh is about to burst with anger.

JOSH: (*to Tali, muttering*) I've got to get out of here.

The hearing continues as he and Tali quietly make their way along the row of seats and out of the room.

BURNSIDE: The wharves are at flashpoint, Your Honour. This court should consider the real-world consequences of its actions.

HAYNE: That, Mr Burnside, is a comment which is liable to be misconstrued as intentionally offensive. This court will not be put under time constraints by you, the MUA or anyone else. The stay is granted and I will hear the full arguments tomorrow morning.

He stands and marches out.

SCENE 39. INT. THE DINING ROOM – JOHN'S HOUSE. NIGHT.

John and his wife have given Corrigan dinner and a goodly amount of red wine.

CORRIGAN: Mediocrity. Enshrined, systemic, celebrated bloody mediocrity. It's all we'll ever have until something ... gives. In Europe it's a matter of pride, even if you're growing tomatoes. Or selling cheese. They're the best tomatoes they can be. The best cheese. In this country it's a criminal offence to try to do something well. Or to ask your employees not to rip off the hand that feeds them in favour of a union that treats them like a bunch of mindless puppets.

JOHN: Chris, I cut my teeth in the newspaper business on IR stories. What you're describing is the culture of the MUA. Always has been.

CORRIGAN: And it's the very culture that makes the whole waterfront a joke.

JOHN: You've come through the bull system, right? Where one bloke starves while the next works, simply on the whim of the manager ... You're going to fix it, aren't you? So that no bloke earns more than another. No one moves ahead, no one gets left behind.

CORRIGAN: That's socialism.

JOHN: Maybe. But for blokes whose fathers and grandfathers walked the hungry mile, it makes sense.

CORRIGAN: Oh, here we go: the history of the waterfront again. These blokes are the highest-paid blue-collar workers in the country. Some of them are earning ninety grand. Because they do unnecessary overtime. Because they do their own rosters and line each other up for leave loadings and penalty rates. The stuff you're talking about is mythology.

JOHN: Myths mean a great deal to the labour movement.

CORRIGAN: Sorry. I don't get it. I never will.

JOHN: That's why you're the man you are, Chris. And John Coombs is the man he is.

Corrigan stands and moves away with his glass of red, restless.

What's that saying? 'The man that can be a worthy enemy will, when reconciled, be a worthier friend'?

Corrigan snorts. Then tries to pull himself out of the black mood.

CORRIGAN: Want to hear something funny? John Coombs has leaked it to his bullyboys that I'm still riding the Vesper, and I've never disabused him of the idea. So I'm getting around on a BMW – which means the poor unsuspecting blighter who bought the Vesper is in for a rude shock if he goes down any dark alleys. Probably should warn the poor sod, I s'pose.

John and his wife laugh. Corrigan, already fairly drunk, takes another large slug of red.

SCENE 40. EXT. THE TOLLGATES – SYDNEY HARBOUR BRIDGE. NIGHT.

Late on a weeknight. The usual amount of Bridge traffic. A red motorbike approaches the tollgates.

The driver is trying to keep the bike upright while digging in his pocket for change. Silver coins scatter onto the ground. And, suddenly, it's all too much – trying to keep the bike upright, trying to find the change – and the bike tilts, tips and slides into the tollbooth, trapping its rider's leg.

It is Corrigan. Despite the pain in his trapped leg and the sheer indignity of his position he can't help but find the whole thing hysterically funny.

TOLL COLLECTOR: Hey, you all right, mate?

Two toll collectors trot towards him. And Corrigan, helmet half on, half off, just lies there, laughing helplessly.

CORRIGAN: Here I am, Coombsie. Come and get me!

SCENE 41. INT. PATRICK HEAD OFFICE. NIGHT.

Corrigan limps into the office guarding his injured leg. To find Paul sitting at a desk writing press releases in the half dark. Paul notices the limp.

PAUL: You all right?

CORRIGAN Rugby injury. Hospital pass.

Paul looks bewildered but lets it go.

PAUL: I've been trying to call you.

Corrigan points to his mobile phone, still sitting in the middle of the table where he left it.

I noticed. The High Court's ordered a stay. And the Prime Minister wants to see you. Tomorrow.

CORRIGAN: It just keeps getting better.

PAUL: I called Freehills to see if they could send Rob with you. Apparently he's on stress leave. My money's on a nervous breakdown.

CORRIGAN: Was it something I said?

SCENE 42. EXT. CANBERRA AIRPORT. DAY.

Chris Corrigan, disguised behind dark sunglasses, climbs into a taxi.

CORRIGAN: Parliament House, please.

The taxi driver does the merest double take, then leans forward and turns up the news as he drives off.

JOURNALIST: (*on the radio*) And Chris Corrigan's brother, Derek, has joined MUA leader John Coombs at a protest rally at Port Botany ...

SCENE 43. EXT. PATRICK DOCK – PORT BOTANY. DAY.

Coombs is addressing a significant gathering of wharfies, supporters and protesters. There are hecklers in the crowd, demanding to know when they can go back to work.

Derek Corrigan stands by nervously awaiting his moment to address the crowd. He has palm cards, his hands are sweaty, his mouth is dry. He takes a nervous sip of water.

COOMBS: We've won in the Federal Court, twice. We'll win in the High Court. It's not a matter of months. Not even a matter of weeks. It could be a matter of days before we're walking through those gates. But patience was always a virtue, comrades ...

Coombs is working very, very hard.

Gwen and Garry are among the onlookers.

GWEN: Come on, Garry. I'll take you home.
GARRY: I'll come later, with Dad.
GWEN: He doesn't know how long he'll be ...
GARRY: I want to stay, Mum. He needs the numbers ...

Gwen sighs. Another stubborn Coombs man ...

Derek Corrigan steps up to the microphone, and promptly bumps his face on it. He stands back, takes a breath, and:

DEREK: I'm delighted to be here to represent the Corrigan family.

A roar of laughter and approval.

SCENE 44. INT. AN ANTECHAMBER – PARLIAMENT HOUSE. DAY.

Corrigan waits in an antechamber. Finally, Peter Reith comes towards him.

REITH: Chris. How're you travelling? Come in. The PM's ready now. For what it's worth, I think he's going to ask where you're getting your legal advice ...

SCENE 45. INT. THE LAUNDRY VAN. NIGHT.

Corrigan bumps away in the back of the laundry van. He is beginning to get very weary.

DEREK: (*voice over*) This particular family has two sides. One is at the top end of town, and the other is at the working-class end of town. My father was working-class through and through. My mother used to walk into the butcher at Mittagong on the Wednesday night before payday ...

SCENE 46. EXT. CORRIGAN'S HOUSE – POINT PIPER. NIGHT.

The laundry van comes down the street, turns into the driveway and into the underground garage. The lights are on in the house.

DEREK: (*voice over*) ... And say, 'What can I get for two and six?' 'Cos that's all she had left to feed a family of six. We ate a lot of kidneys ...

SCENE 47. INT. THE HALLWAY – CORRIGAN'S HOUSE. NIGHT.

Corrigan walks in, still limping slightly, to find Valerie coming down the stairs towards him. They hug.

VALERIE: How are you?
CORRIGAN: Bloody awful.

Lucy trots down the stairs, followed with more restraint and decorum, as befits a thirteen-year-old, by Joseph. Chris hugs Lucy. General hellos and welcome-backs and we-missed-yous.

Corrigan's relief at his family's return is palpable.

SCENE 48. INT. THE LIVING ROOM – CORRIGAN'S HOUSE. NIGHT.

Corrigan and Valerie sit over coffee or brandy, talking quietly. It is late. A newspaper lies on the table with the headline: 'Corrigan brother speaks out: He couldn't lay straight in bed'.

CORRIGAN: I feel like the whole bloody thing's turning to shit around me. The banks are spineless. The Government's getting shaky. The public thinks I'm Satan. And my alleged colleagues in the corporate community have just gone up in smoke. Not a word ... not a fax, not a phone call. And, if I happen to see any of them in passing, its like I've stepped in dog shit. 'You go out there and be the punching bag, Chris. We're right behind you, mate.' Am I the only one left with any guts? Or have I lost the plot?
VALERIE: I thought the Government was on your side.
CORRIGAN: Oh, Reith's a fighter. But in the end they're on their own side. (*Indicating the 'Corrigan brother' headline*) And he's bloody everywhere you look. Banging on about solidarity and the common man. Fat lot of solidarity he showed when

he dumped poor old Mum and Dad in the middle of this. He'll probably be outside the High Court tomorrow with a bloody sandwich board. Misspelt at that.

A moment.

Starting to think the only bloke with any integrity in the whole cesspool is the one I'm trying to knock over.

He looks carefully at Valerie – she's tired from the long-haul flight.

I haven't even asked about Italy.

VALERIE: It's still there. And Dario's donkey …

CORRIGAN *and* VALERIE: … Had a foal …

CORRIGAN: You should go to bed. You're jetlagged.

VALERIE: My body clock thinks it's lunchtime. Let's go dancing.

CORRIGAN: Great. We could go in the camouflaged vehicle.

Valerie smiles – the old wry sense of humour hasn't left him yet.

SCENE 49. EXT. CORRIGAN'S HOUSE – POINT PIPER. DAY.

Joseph and Lucy Corrigan, in school uniforms, are ushered into a dark car by a security guard who then climbs in with them. The car takes off.

SCENE 50. INT. THE STUDY, HALLWAY AND BATHROOM – CORRIGAN'S HOUSE. DAY.

Valerie is tapping away on a laptop computer, concentrating on a report for the Planning and Development Committee of Woollahra Council. The radio is on so that she can listen to Corrigan doing a phone interview.

CORRIGAN: (*on the radio*) … Seem to think I went into this and risked the best part of sixty million dollars for a lark. I have a plan, a comprehensive and detailed plan about how to operate both my business and the waterfront.

INTERVIEWER: (*on the radio*) Chris Corrigan there. And next on AM ...

The phone rings. She watches it for a moment, wary.

VALERIE Chris? Are you getting that?

No answer. Valerie moves to the phone.

Hello. Valerie Corrigan.

The other caller is just a male-voiced murmur. It is brutal, violent, taunting. Only snatches are audible: '... fuck ... kids ... arses cover your little angels in shit ...' Valerie listens for a moment, then puts the phone down.

She moves to the bathroom and vomits into the toilet. Then she wipes her face, flushes the toilet, rinses her mouth.

And prepares to get on with the day. Corrigan comes down the stairs checking his mobile phone for messages, shrugging on his jacket, hurrying.

CORRIGAN: Who was that on the phone?

VALERIE: Just Bec. Organising my life, as usual.

He knows she's probably lying. It's tacit between them – she does not tell him and he does not ask.

SCENE 51. INT. THE KITCHEN – TULLYS' HOUSE. DAY.

A phone sitting on a side table. Widen to reveal Tony Tully, sitting beside it, his face dark.

He stands and walks out, slamming the back door behind him.

SCENE 52. INT. THE HIGH COURT – CANBERRA. DAY.

May 4th, 1998. A rabble of media, cameras, microphones. Observers, participants, protesters. The legal teams make their way through and into the court.

SCENE 53. INT. AN ANTECHAMBER – THE HIGH COURT. DAY.

Burnside puffs on a rollie cigarette as he quietly arranges and rearranges the sticky tabs on his briefing document. He closes his eyes for a moment, breathing deeply, getting into the zone.

Josh appears silently in the doorway, just checking.

SCENE 54. INT. THE HIGH COURT – CANBERRA. DAY.

The packed courtroom gets to its feet as not one, not two, not three – but all seven High Court judges file into the court. The faces of several of the journalists: 'Fuck …'

FEMALE ABC JOURNALIST: (*voice over*) And for the first time in its ninety-seven-year history all seven High Court judges will hear Patrick's request for special leave to appeal …

What follows is a series of very rapid scenes linked by cuts to the swelling crowds both outside the High Court and on the waterfront.

SCENE 55. EXT. MAIN GATE – WEBB DOCK. DAY.

Protesters chanting: 'The workers … united … will never be defeated'. The sound of news helicopters above them.

On the ground, Tony Tully throws a cup of hot coffee – or urine – at the face of the nearest security guard.

SCENE 56. INT. THE HIGH COURT – CANBERRA. DAY.

Roger Gyles, QC, is on his feet representing Patrick.

GYLES: … Effectively looking at a union monopoly on the waterfront. If, for example, the Labor Party were to win at the upcoming election, it could very well become impossible for the stevedoring companies to hire non-union labour ... We submit that, with the Federal election only months away, the Court should not interfere with the status quo ...

Justice Brennan turns his body side-on to Gyles.

JUSTICE BRENNAN: Frankly, I find that remark deeply offensive. I will not accept the submission ...

The tiniest of smiles twitches at the corners of Burnside's mouth.

SCENE 57. INT. THE HIGH COURT – CANBERRA. DAY.

Burnside is on his feet.

BURNSIDE: ... All of those ranged against us say that this court is powerless to do anything but watch Patrick count the dead and bayonet the wounded ... We say the court has ample power to prevent the last step in this conspiracy being played out ...

Watching him, once again Josh has tears of admiration in his eyes.

SCENE 58. EXT. THE CITY – SYDNEY. DAY.

A high view of Sydney. It has been raining. The city is covered in a blanket of mist, as though all of Sydney – indeed, the whole country – is awaiting the outcome of this court case.

SCENE 59. EXT. MAIN GATE – PATRICK PORT BOTANY DOCK. DAY.

It has been raining at Port Botany. Wharfies and protesters have found shelter anywhere they can. There's a strange mood – as though they are in suspended animation – and a fear that the rain may in some way be symbolic.

This moment is attenuated, somehow, by the faces of the men, the trade union banners limp and dripping, the red paint of the 'MUA HERE TO STAY' posters running in rivulets and dripping off the edges.

John Coombs, Gwen, Garry and as many others as can fit are crowded around a television set under the sopping awning of a tent.

FEMALE ABC JOURNALIST: (*on television*) In a lengthy, complex and very qualified statement, it is clear that six of the seven High Court judges have upheld Justice Tony North's judgement and found in favour of the Maritime Union ...

There are whoops and leaps of joy. Only John Coombs stays in his seat. He's pleased, he's smiling – but he knows it's a long way from over.

All around him, exuberant celebrations. 'Solidarity Forever' rings out.

Cut to black.

SCENE 60. INT. CORRIGAN'S OFFICE – PATRICK HEAD OFFICE. DAY.

Corrigan is staring out the rain-spattered window, talking quietly on the phone. Sundry staff and advisors hover anxiously around outside the open door.

Snatches of Corrigan's words are audible:

CORRIGAN: So, that's the part Jon English did, is it? Good for you. Great news.

From the television in the next room come the strains of 'Solidarity Forever'.

Corrigan's secretary looks at Paul. This is very odd behaviour from a man who has probably just lost hundreds of millions of dollars.

JENNY: Who's he talking to?

PAUL: His son. The school's doing Pirates of Penzance. Joe got the lead.

CORRIGAN: (*muted*) ... Is that the one with yah-yah 'Modern Major General' in it? Or is that Pinafore?

SCENE 61. EXT. MAIN GATE – PATRICK PORT BOTANY DOCK. DAY.

The celebrations are continuing at Port Botany. A lot of very happy – and very wet – wharfies, unionists and supporters.

RADIO REPORTER: (*voice over*) At first sight this looked like a clear victory for the Maritime Union, but the discretionary powers of the high court have somewhat blurred the issue …

SCENE 62. INT. COOMBS' OFFICE – MUA. DAY.

John Coombs is listening to the radio. His face is darkening.

RADIO REPORTER: (*voice over*) … The court has left the ultimate decision in the hands of the administrators who, if unable to trade, will have no choice but to wind up the companies. This means the union workers will be unable to reclaim their jobs …

SCENE 63. INT. COMBET'S OFFICE – ACTU. DAY.

Greg Combet is also listening to the radio.

RADIO REPORTER: (*voice over*) … Chris Corrigan and the Government may achieve the outcome they wanted, almost by default . The Minister for Workplace Relations, Peter Reith, is confident …

REITH: (*voice over*) There's a lot of love in Canberra today …

Combet looks as though he could vomit.

SCENE 64. INT. COOMBS' OFFICE – MUA. DAY.

Coombs is virtually shouting down the phone.

COOMBS: What is going on? The press are saying the administrators are going to wind the companies up. I've gone public saying we're going back to work.

Cross-cut as required with:

SCENE 65. INT. MELBOURNE AIRPORT. DAY.

Josh, standing with Burnside in the middle of Melbourne airport, is too stunned to speak.

JOSH: John, I ... We did win ...

SCENE 66. INT. THE BOARDROOM – ACTU. DAY.

Bill Kelty is red in the face and deeply distressed.

KELTY: I knew we shouldn't've relied on fucking lawyers. Trade Unions fight industrially.

COMBET: You said it was my call, Bill.

KELTY: Yeah, and if it's failed, then we have to pull the big bang. Whether you and Coombs like it or not.

SCENE 67. INT. COOMBS' OFFICE – MUA. DAY.

Back to Coombs and Josh.

COOMBS: That's why Peter Reith's twittering like a lovebird, is it? Because he's lost?

Cross-cut as required with:

SCENE 68. INT. MELBOURNE AIRPORT. DAY.

JOSH: John, it's a spin. For the media. They can't admit they've lost ...

COOMBS: If you've sold me a pup on this, mate, and I've sold the members a pup because of it, you're sacked and we won't be paying a cent of your fees ... I've got fourteen hundred men who've been standing out there for three weeks, rain, hail or bloody cyclone. Living on a miserable bloody two hundred bucks a week we get passing the hat round the unions. And they think they're going back to work tomorrow. What do you suggest I tell 'em?

JOSH: John, they can't be expected to understand the intricacies –

COOMBS: How can they understand it if I can't bloody understand it myself? It's your job, mate. Your bloody job. Why else am I paying you five hundred dollars an hour?

SCENE 69. INT. THE BOARDROOM – ACTU. DAY.

KELTY: This is a cock-up. A fucking expensive bloody cock up.

SCENE 70. INT. PATRICK HEAD OFFICE. DAY.

The office is now empty. Corrigan stands still. Looks around. Moves to another vantage point. Now that he is alone his utter devastation is apparent.

The television is on in the corner. On it, John Coombs is talking about his workers needing jobs – blokes with wives and kids to support.

COOMBS: (*on television*) ... All they want, all they've ever wanted, is their jobs. They've got families, these blokes. They've got wives and kids to feed and clothe and educate. They've been living on handouts for weeks now – months, some of 'em. And now they're brave enough to say they'll work for nothing. Just to get back their basic right to do a day's work for a day's pay ...

CORRIGAN: What about the other four hundred blokes, John? The 'scabs'? They've got wives and kids too.

He hears a discreet cough from a corner of the room. It's Paul, sitting quietly, just checking that he's okay. Corrigan nods to Coombs.

People call him a chardonnay socialist. But the real reason he planted those grapes down on the farm was to give his son in the wheelchair something to do.

He stares at Coombs, almost as though he's talking to him.

It wasn't personal. I never wanted to put him through this.

The mobile phone sits in the middle of the table. Can he face doing what he now realises is his only option?

SCENE 71. EXT. PATRICK HEAD OFFICE. EVENING.

Corrigan walks out of the building – to be ambushed by the media. Cameras, microphones, the usual hullaballoo.

SYDNEY JOURNALIST 1: Mr Corrigan, have you sacked your lawyers yet?

CORRIGAN: Not yet.

SYDNEY JOURNALIST 2: We understand Lindsay Fox is standing by to take over Patrick. What do you say to that?

CORRIGAN: You can tell Mr Fox that when I need a truck driver I'll call him.

SYDNEY JOURNALIST 3: Your share price is at an all-time low. You're staring down the barrel of bankruptcy. And there's still no chance you're preparing to jettison Patrick?

CORRIGAN: That's right, Mike. No chance.

SYDNEY JOURNALIST 2: What's going to happen to the non-union workers on the docks, Mr Corrigan? Will you be sacking them?

SCENE 72. INT. THE LIVING ROOM – CORRIGAN'S HOUSE. NIGHT.

Corrigan walks in. He is close to ashen with exhaustion. Joe appears out of nowhere. And, in a perfect parody of his father:

JOE: That's right, Mike. No chance.

Valerie calls from another room.

VALERIE: Sit.

Corrigan puts his bag down, and does. Lucy carefully carries in a cup of tea or coffee and hands it to him.

CORRIGAN: Thanks, Luce.

To his mild surprise she plonks herself on his knee.

JOE: And another thing, Mike. Did I ever mention about cutting celery at three o'clock in the morning? It's very character building, you know.

And Corrigan actually laughs.

The Corrigans at home. Above: Chris (Geoff Morrell) and Valerie (Helen Thomson). Below: Lucy (Ashleigh Millo), Chris (Geoff Morrell) and Joseph (Louis Corbett).

SCENE 73. INT. THE LIVING ROOM – COOMBS' HOUSE. NIGHT.

Coombs' mobile phone is ringing in the lounge room. Coombs comes racing in from outside. He's out of breath when he answers the phone.

COOMBS: John Coombs.

Cross-cut as required with:

SCENE 74. INT. THE HALLWAY – CORRIGAN'S HOUSE. NIGHT.

CORRIGAN: John. Chris Corrigan.

Coombs nearly falls over.

He looks up to see Gwen has appeared in the doorway. Somehow, she knows this call is momentous.

COOMBS: Yes?

CORRIGAN: I think we should meet.

A long pause. Both men can hear each other's breathing down the phone line.

COOMBS: I thought you'd never ask.

SCENE 75. EXT. MAIN GATE – WEBB DOCK. DAY.

May 7th, 1998. A red carpet is rolled out leading to the main entry gate to the docks.

Cut to:

A bus carrying the last load of 'scabs' moves out the gates. It is undisturbed by the protesters. Inside, some of the faces of these men: angry, bewildered, betrayed.

Cut to:

Sean is addressing a throng of people.

SEAN: ... And last but not least, this bloke. Our lawyer. Worth his weight in gold bloody bullion ...

He climbs down from a milk crate and hands over to Josh. Josh climbs onto the crate, shivering in his lawyer's suit on a bitterly cold Melbourne morning. Among those watching him are Sean, Tony, Brendan, Cherie, Lyn, Podge, Nuts and Chopper.

JOSH: Last minute legal advice, but first: you guys are fucking heroes. And I am unbelievably proud to have served you. But it's not over: you need to hold discipline. If you encounter a scab, if a security guard spits on you, if a manager provokes you, do not retaliate. This victory of ours is poised on a knife-edge. The country is behind you – but only if you prove you deserve their support. So, go to it, guys. Long live the MUA.

There's a round of applause for Josh. And Brendan hugs Sean tightly.

BRENDAN: Thanks, mate. Thanks a lot.

SEAN: Thought you thought unions were bullshit.

Brendan gives him a playful punch in the gut.

SCENE 76. EXT. PATRICK PORT BOTANY DOCK. DAY.

At Port Botany John Coombs marches ahead of the men, Gwen beside him. Halfway along the red carpet a cluster of Maltese workers lifts him onto their shoulders and parades him like a conquering hero.

SCENE 77. EXT. MAIN GATE – WEBB DOCK. DAY.

Josh and Sean are standing at the side, watching as the men walk through, back to work. They go in single file. Jennie George marches with them and several around her do the cha-cha as they go. A bloke from the Meatworkers' Union hands Josh his bluey. Josh takes a moment away from his mobile.

JOSH: Cheers, mate. Thanks a lot. (*Into his mobile*) They're going through now, mate. This is … just … fucking … incredible …

SCENE 78. INT. A PODIATRIST'S SURGERY. DAY.

A podiatrist is watching young Anna Combet walk back and forth, feeling her shoes, checking the innersoles.

Greg looks on. But his mobile phone is glued to his ear and he's mighty choked up.

COMBET: Yep. Yep. I can hear ...

He looks up to Anna and the podiatrist, embarrassed by his emotion.

Sorry ...

SCENE 79. EXT. MAIN GATE – PATRICK PORT BOTANY DOCK. DAY.

John Coombs standing at the side, watching the men go through the gates. Gwen is with him, and Garry, and various other members of the Coombs family. Coombs is having immense difficulty controlling his emotions.

GWEN: It's all right, love. It's over. You've won.
COOMBS: It's not over, Gwennie. Nowhere near.

SCENE 80. INT./EXT. SEAN'S HORSE FLOAT – WEBB DOCK. DAY.

The celebration continues outside as Sean packs up his belongings. Not much – some clothes, his mobile phone, a few books. And the Gorby matriushka doll.

His final gesture is to cross off the final day on the wall of the float. Day 99.

SCENE 81. INT. THE HALLWAY AND KITCHEN – SEAN'S HOUSE. DAY.

Sean walks in to the empty house. But, bit by bit, he becomes aware of the presence of others:

A collection of grocery-filled plastic shopping bags in the kitchen.

Bits and pieces of small child's clothing leading in a trail to the bathroom. There's the sound of a child splashing and singing tunelessly in the bath.

SEAN: Hello?

ALEX: (*out of view, from the bathroom*) Dad. Come and look. I can stay underwater for a whole minute ...

Janine appears from out the back, a washing basket in her hands.

JANINE: Hi.

ALEX: Da-ad ...

JANINE: Just a second, Alex. Shhh, now, Nicky's asleep.

Sean is struggling to adjust.

SEAN: Does this mean you're back?

JANINE: I thought we could try for ... what's that thing John Coombs is doing? – a 'negotiated settlement'.

SCENE 82. EXT. THE BACKYARD – SEAN'S HOUSE. NIGHT.

It's cold. Sean and Janine pull jackets tightly around them as they inspect the state of the backyard. The grass is overgrown. The small above-ground swimming pool is filled with leaves and other debris.

JANINE: If I'd known how long you were going to be stuck down there I'd've moved back in. Mum was starting to drive me dippy. Christ, there's mould in there we could sell to science.

Sean touches her freezing hands, gives them a rub. Their breath blows steam into the night air.

SEAN: Come on. You're freezing.

JANINE: Wait. I want to ... In the beer garden – that day. There was something about the way the light was hitting your eyes. You used to look kind of callow, you know, still learning. But you looked grown up.

SEAN: Thanks very much ...

JANINE: Let me finish ... The night of the big picket, I watched you from behind, with your loudhailer. You looked – the set of your neck, your shoulders – the way grown-up men used to look when you were a kid, you know? All the fathers and uncles and schoolteachers and priests. All those people trusted you. And I just kept seeing it – your neck and your shoulders and all those people trusting you. And I thought: I want that. I want my sons to have that.

While he listens Sean's fingers have been describing circles in the murky surface of the pool. The ripples expand. Somehow, in the silence of the night, and the expanse of the sky, and those ripples on the surface of the pool, this is more than one woman speaking to one man. Janine is speaking for all the women in this story, to all the men.

Fade to black.

SCENE 83. EXT. PATRICK'S MELBOURNE DOCK. DAY.

Coombs walks with Sean across the expanse of the dock. It gives him real pleasure to see the men in the cranes, in the straddles, doing the lashing on the ships. Although they are now all wearing regulation blue and yellow 'Patrick' vests they are still his men.

A cluster of blokes is coming off shift, dragging off helmets and vests. Among them are Tony and Brendan. They surround Coombs and Sean and give them a huge cheer. There's much hugging and backslapping and good-natured chiacking. Coombs is their hero.

TONY: Hey, Coombsie. Corrigan might've put his filthy label on us, but we're still your blokes ...

COOMBS: This is his idea of a fashion statement, is it? Always did have lousy taste. How're things?

BRENDAN: Dandy. All the stuff in our lockers was trashed. The supervisors walk through our room any time they like. Can the union do anything about that?

COOMBS: Softly softly catchee monkey, mate.

TONY: There's a lot of talk, Coombsie. They reckon a lot of blokes are going to get the handshake. Even though we beat the prick fair and square.

Coombs avoids Sean's look.

COOMBS: Yeah. A few. Not sure yet.

SCENE 84. INT. THE BOARDROOM – MUA. DAY.

Super caption: 'May ...'

John Coombs and Greg Combet are waiting. Coombs is pacing around, Combet lounging restlessly against the window frame.

COOMBS: Where the blazes is he? He said ten.

COMBET: Playing the tactical advantage.

COOMBS: I'll tactical advantage him. We won this thing, not him ...

With which Chris Corrigan walks into the boardroom. He is dressed casually, wearing a particularly bright green jumper and carrying his bike helmet.

A moment while all three check each other out – who looks weaker, more battered, closer to defeat.

CORRIGAN: (*indicating Combet*) I see you've brought the cavalry.

COMBET: Chris.

Corrigan puts his hand out to shake. First Coombs' hand. Then Combet's.

Silence as all three pull out chairs to sit down. The body language tells many stories. All three half expect to be walking out at any second.

Okay. Can we make this work or what?

CORRIGAN: My share price is a dollar eighteen. I'm on the nose with the shipping companies. I've lost market share to P and O, so I couldn't pay your blokes even if I wanted to. There are going to be redundancies and the Government won't pay them unless they see reform. The banks could knock me over any day and, believe me, nothing would make them happier.

They're lining up another buyer, and if that happens, you really think they'll employ union men? So, at the risk of stating the obvious, I'm fucked. And if I'm fucked, so are you.

Corrigan's old wry humour.

Moral of the story? Love the one you're with.

He slides a single piece of A4 paper across the desk. Combet picks it up.

COMBET: This your wish list is it, Chris?

He lays it on the table so that both he and Coombs can see it. It reads:

'Agreed no. of redundancies

No three for two practice

Contract out maintenance

Management control rosters

Aggregate wage

Casuals in preference to overtime'.

John? Can we work with that?

Silence while Coombs struggles to control his alarm at the extent of Corrigan's demands. Then he puts his cards on the table.

COOMBS: Voluntary redundancy only. Entitlements paid in full. A collective agreement. No individual contracts. The scabs go. And Patrick stays a union operation. That's not negotiable.

Another silence while Corrigan assesses.

How many redundancies are we looking at?

CORRIGAN: At a guess – rough estimate ... seven hundred.

Coombs, already volatile, is nearly apoplectic.

COOMBS: You're fucking kidding, aren't you? That's half the workforce.

Coombs swallows hard in response to Combet's look: stay calm.

CORRIGAN: If this is an ambush to tell me you won't budge, I'm out of here.

He's on his feet. Silence.

COOMBS: Oh, for Christ's sake, Chris, sit down. And take off that bloody jumper before we all go blind. Struth, with all your millions, wouldn't you think you could buy a decent pullover?

SCENE 85. INT. THE BOARDROOM – PATRICK HEAD OFFICE. DAY.

Super caption: 'June'.

Coombs, Combet and Corrigan in negotiation.

CORRIGAN: When hell freezes over.

He's laughing. Combet's cajoling.

COMBET: Seven mill' for our trade practices fines, one point eight for our legals. Come on, Chris. It's a drop in the ocean compared to the productivity gains you claim you're going to make …

Corrigan is silent.

Little bird tells me your friends at the banks are getting pretty toey …

CORRIGAN: My lawyers advise me –

And Combet is suddenly on his feet, thumping the table, towering over Corrigan. Exploiting the element of surprise.

COMBET: Your lawyers are a bunch of grubs. If I thought we were going to be arguing about what your lawyers think, I wouldn't've got out of bed …

And he turns and begins to walk out of the room. He's almost there. His hand is on the doorknob …

CORRIGAN: I'll pay it.

Combet turns back and quietly resumes his seat.

SCENE 86. INT. A LIFT – PATRICK HEAD OFFICE. DAY.

Coombs and Combet walk out of the lift.

COMBET: Negotiations are like one-night stands. Always go to their place so you can be the one to walk out.

Coombs snorts with laughter. For a moment this is hilarious, but the laughter goes on just a bit too long, as though the man is coming close to hysteria.

COOMBS: How am I going to find seven hundred who want to go?

Combet realises just how distressed Coombs really is.

SCENE 87. INT. THE HALLWAY – CORRIGAN'S HOUSE. NIGHT.

Super caption: 'July'.

The phone is ringing in the Corrigan house. Joe and Lucy race each other to answer it. Then stop cold – and glance at their mother. Is it safe to answer the phone now? Valerie nods. The race is back on. Joe gets there first.

JOE: Corrigan residence? Oh ... Yes ... He's here.

Corrigan, dressed casually – it's Sunday night after all – takes the phone.

CORRIGAN: Chris Corrigan ... What? Now? ... Give me an hour ...

He hangs up and turns to Valerie.

The banks want to see me. I think this might be the end of the line, Val.

JOE: 'Sokay, Dad. We'll go and cut celery as a family ...

Joe has his father's sense of humour.

SCENE 88. INT. A CORPORATE BOARDROOM. NIGHT.

Corrigan walks in to the boardroom flanked by his minder Paul. Ranged around the huge table are up to 50 men in suits. It's a total ambush. Corrigan summons every bit of bravado he can muster.

CORRIGAN: Is this when everyone jumps out and says 'Surprise'? Or am I on *This is Your Life?*

BANKER: Sit down, Chris. Can we get you a drink?

CORRIGAN: You can get to the point.

BANKER: We've been extraordinarily patient with Patrick's difficulties. But there comes a point ... You gave your word in early April that this would be over in a month. It's been nearly four. Not to mention John Coombs threatening to join the banks in the union's conspiracy action. We can't afford that kind of publicity, Chris. We want you to settle. Now.

CORRIGAN: I'm halfway through the negotiation. We're making progress. I can get more ... Has Coombs been talking to you blokes?

BANKER: No one's been talking to us. We just want it over. Banks are on the nose with the public anyway, as you well know. An awful lot of the public are members of unions. We can't take the risk of the unions pulling their super funds out.

CORRIGAN: And if I don't?

BANKER: We are legally entitled to withdraw our funds. Two hundred and fifty mill'. Give or take.

And suddenly the famous Corrigan temper is on display.

CORRIGAN: You've got to be fucking joking, haven't you? How dare you call me here in the middle of the night – ('to face some kind of star chamber ...')

Paul – quite literally – starts to drag him from the room.

PAUL: Chris ... Come on. Chris ... (*To the others*) Give us a minute, will you?

SCENE 89. EXT. A CORPORATE CORRIDOR. NIGHT.

Corrigan and Paul at the end of a long corridor.

PAUL: Chris, they've got you by the balls. You could lose the lot. Patrick. Lang. Your house. How's Val going to feel about that?

SCENE 90. INT. THE CORPORATE BOARDROOM. NIGHT.

Corrigan and Paul re-enter and take their seats.

CORRIGAN: We've considered your position and our answer remains the same. I will not settle until I've pushed this negotiation as far as it'll go.

And the temper erupts again.

I've come this far. I've been hung out to dry in every newspaper and TV station in the country. I've been accused of being a liar, a cheat and the nearest thing to a fucking paedophile. My family's been subjected to every kind of threat imaginable. And you seriously think I'll kowtow to a bunch of David Jones mannequins in a boardroom? I am not going to be dragged out at nine o'clock on a Sunday night to be ambushed by a roomful of spineless sycophants I've never laid eyes on in my life. If you want to foreclose on me, go right ahead. Be my guest. Send me to the wall. But I'm fucked if I'll leave the job half done because you lot haven't got the guts to see it through.

SCENE 91. EXT. PATRICK DOCK – PORT BOTANY. NIGHT.

The docks are lit up and working night shift as usual – a ship is in. Cranes are operating; straddles and forklifts dart back and forth.

A dark car, driven by Frank the security guard, pulls up.

Corrigan climbs out and stands, just looking at the docks operating. Smooth, efficient. His work. And he stands to lose the lot.

And, before Frank can gather his wits, Corrigan walks up to the security gate.

FRANK: Jesus …

… Nods to the security officer – who nearly falls over when he

sees who he is allowing through – and walks out, and out, onto the apron of the dock …

And keeps walking. Almost as though, by his sheer presence, he is saying, 'Here I am. Come and get me'.

A bloke in a straddle looks up. His eyes nearly pop out of his head: a tall, lanky man, with glasses, in a suit. Standing, completely alone, in the middle of the dock. The straddle driver leans forward to speak into his microphone.

Corrigan sees this. And as he looks around he sees attention spreading from one straddle driver to another, to another. He sees faces looking down out of cranes.

And he just stands there. And waits.

Frank, running after Corrigan, stops dead as he sees:

As though falling from the sky, a huge container … It falls … falls… and lands with a ear-splitting thud.

Corrigan opens his eyes a crack. The container, no more than a few metres from his face, is emblazoned: 'PATRICK'.

He opens his eyes some more. And breathes. He's still standing.

SCENE 92. INT. COOMBS' OFFICE – MUA. DAY.

Coombs is sitting at his desk. As though in some kind of paralysis of exhaustion. A secretary pops her head in the door.

MUA SECRETARY: John. Chris Corrigan wants you to call him. It's urgent. He – um – he sounded upset.

Coombs nods. But does not reach for the phone. Instead, he reaches for his jacket.

SCENE 93. INT. COMBET'S OFFICE – ACTU. DAY.

Combet is listening to a caller on his mobile. Concerned.

SCENE 94. INT. CORRIGAN'S OFFICE – PATRICK HEAD OFFICE. DAY.

CORRIGAN: (*into the phone*) I can't reach Coombs. This is not a joke. The banks are foreclosing close of business Thursday. This deal is going to fall over.

SCENE 95. INT. THE BOARDROOM – ACTU. DAY.

Teams of negotiators from both sides are arriving: Corrigan, his finance officer, his solicitors; Combet, Josh, Burnside.

Josh leans in to Combet.

JOSH: Where's John?

Combet quietly leaves the room as the others continue to take their seats and arrange their files.

SCENE 96. EXT. A PICKET LINE. DAY.

Coombs is on a picket line, talking on his mobile phone.

COOMBS: I'm on another picket line. Storemen and packers. Can't get enough of the things.

Cross-cut as required with:

SCENE 97. INT. COMBET'S OFFICE – ACTU. DAY.

COMBET: (*into the phone*) John. I need you here. We've got to lock down this negotiation.

COOMBS: These blokes supported us. We'd've been history without the other unions. I've got to return the favour.

COMBET: John, you're talking like –

COOMBS: I don't break my promises, mate. That's what solidarity's about.

SCENE 98. INT. THE BEDROOM – COOMBS' HOUSE. NIGHT.

Coombs lies in bed, awake. Gwen sleeps beside him.

SCENE 99. INT. COOMBS' OFFICE – MUA. DAY.

Coombs drags his mobile phone from his pocket. Reminiscent of Corrigan facing the phone call he knew he had to make.

SCENE 100. INT. COMBET'S OFFICE – ACTU. DAY.

Cut to Combet, but not in direct continuity; further into what is a very, very volatile conversation.

COMBET: (*into the phone*) John, if Corrigan goes under all the jobs are gone.

Cross-cut as required with:

SCENE 101. INT. COOMBS' OFFICE – MUA. DAY.

COOMBS: (*into the phone*) So … ? Someone else takes over Patrick. Someone we can deal with.

COMBET: You're dreaming, mate. A new operator won't deal with us. Corrigan is.

COOMBS: Maintenance, Greg. That's two hundred jobs. No-one wants a settlement more than me. But how are they going to see it? A deal where half of them go; and the rest sit in cranes four hours at a stretch, pissing in bottles … How am I going to sell this, Greg?

COMBET: Mate, if anyone can sell it, you can.

COOMBS: Oh, don't fuckin' sweet-talk me. I've never had a bloke sacked. I've always moved 'em, found 'em somewhere else safe. Not one bloke. They trust me. You know as well as I do, a union leader who can't get a deal up with the membership is dead meat.

COMBET: John, you have withstood the full force of the most rapacious capitalist we've ever had in this industry –

COOMBS: Oh, bull …

COMBET: … In bed with a government that's using its entire arsenal to wipe the union movement off the map. The fact that the MUA's still standing is a fucking miracle. You have saved your union. Mate, you'll be fucking immortalised.

COOMBS: 'We knocked Corrigan out in three courts'. That's what they're going to say. 'So why are we losing conditions we won in the sixties and seventies?'

COMBET: So tell them the truth.

Silence.

We should've lost them years ago. I know it. You know it. Chris Corrigan knows it.

A brief silence.

John. Listen to me. The scabs are gone. The redundancies are voluntary. The entitlements are paid. The costs are paid. There's no individual contracts. There's a new EA with a productivity bonus on our terms. And the single most important thing: those men on the docks are loyal, card-carrying, proud members of the MUA. And no one can take that away from you. MUA, here to stay.

COOMBS: Half the MUA, mate. Half.

COMBET: And the rest have their dignity intact and a hundred and fifty million worth of entitlements to prove it.

Silence.

Change hurts, John.

COOMBS: Always the big-picture man …

COMBET: The MUA's where I learned to look at the big picture. I learned it from people like you.

Silence again. Coombs is dangerously close to tears.

What did you say to me at the beginning of all this?

COOMBS: 'I run the union'.

COMBET: 'Stand or fall. Win or lose. I run the union'. We're out of time, John. You have to make a call.

Silence from Coombs.

I've been beside you every step of the way, mate. But now

it's down to you. The banks are foreclosing five o'clock today. Make the call.

A long, long silence.

COOMBS: This is killing me, Greg.

Combet waits.

Settle it.

Cut to black.

SCENE 102. INT. THE MEETING ROOM – MUA. DAY.

A series of rapid grabs of the stop-work meeting. Combet is there. And Josh, who is aghast at the violent intensity of it. Sean, Tony, Brendan.

But it is Coombs who bears the brunt. Men shout at him, and each other, both for and against the settlement: 'We fuckin' trusted you, Coombsie', 'What about the casuals? We're stuck doing the lashings', 'Why don't you all shut up and let the poor man speak? He's saved our bacon, you morons', 'I can't pay the mortgage if I don't do overtime', 'What about the maintenance blokes? They're stuffed', 'What's the point of a union if it's going to sell you down the river?', 'Without the union we'd all be stuffed, ya fuckwit'.

And so on.

Tony Tully is particularly vocal. One nuggety Maltese man marches up to Coombs and rolls up his sleeves as though to have fisticuffs. With which a second Maltese bloke hauls the first aside, marches up to Coombs – perhaps he's going to hit him – and instead embraces him so tightly Coombs looks like he will asphyxiate.

Dissolve to:

A sea of hands in the air, voting up the settlement. A spontaneous wave of applause. And a moist-eyed Combet wraps his arms around a dazed John Coombs.

COMBET: You did it, mate. I don't know how you did it, but you did it.

SCENE 103. EXT. FEDERAL COURT – MELBOURNE. DAY.

Josh and Burnside walk towards the Federal Court.

Josh stops in the doorway.

JOSH: Um. Julian, do you mind? I just want to be by myself for a few minutes. Just to kiss my beautiful conspiracy case goodbye.

Burnside understands. He slips inside the court. Josh wanders a few paces. Sits himself down on the court steps, holding his piles of files in his hand as though they were the gold-inlaid leaves of the Book of Kells.

SCENE 104. INT. LIMBO. DAY.

JOSH: People say it would have gone on for years – with stays and adjournments and appeals – would've bankrupted the union. But any government that covertly supports the mass sacking of workers simply because they are members of a union should not stand. I know we would have won it. We would have brought down this government. And wouldn't that've been a service to humanity?

SCENE 105. INT. THE BOARDROOM – MUA. DAY.

Super caption: 'August'.

John Coombs, Greg Combet, Josh Bornstein; Chris Corrigan, Paul, Corrigan's solicitor.

An incredibly solemn, silent moment, as Coombs and Corrigan, on behalf of the MUA and Patrick Stevedores, sign the settlement documents.

COMBET: There would have been another way of achieving this, Chris, if you'd just had patience.

CORRIGAN: There wasn't, and you know it. No one willingly concedes power. It has to be taken. If you'd been me, what would you have done?

A long moment.

COMBET: I wouldn't be you for quids.

Cut to black.

Super caption: 'One year later'.

SCENE 106. EXT. PATRICK'S MELBOURNE DOCK. DAY.

Very early morning and the first shift of the day is arriving. But they're arriving with company: Brendan Tully, Podge, Chopper, Nuts and sundry others. And each one has a dog on a leash.

There are Rottweilers, German shepherds, schnauzers, Pekinese, poodles, common or garden kelpies and cattle dogs, the odd English sheep dog and even a few poodles and fluffy white things. Many of them are wearing doggy jackets emblazoned with the words 'MUA HERE TO STAY'.

BURNSIDE: (*voice over*) It's fitting that on the anniversary of the events that began it all – on the day that every wharfie in the country has begged, borrowed or stolen a canine mascot to commemorate the dogs and the shitsticks of that fateful night – we celebrate the career of one of the dispute's heroes ...

SCENE 107. INT./EXT. A WATERSIDE PUB. DAY.

The retirement function for John Coombs. All of the Union personnel are present, most with wives or partners: Greg Combet and Petra, Burnside, Josh, Sean and Janine, Gwen and Garry Coombs and the rest of the Coombs family. Hanging around the periphery, half-in-half-out of the gate, many with their dogs, are a number of the wharfies, including Brendan Tully.

BURNSIDE: ... And, frankly, one of mine. This case still remains my biggest victory. And in the words of the six-foot-four Samoan janitor who spoke to us after the High Court win:

'Thanks, mate. Now we all feel a bit safer'. I give you John Coombs.

Somewhere in the audience, Josh mutters to himself.

JOSH: Julian. You're a fucking Bolshevik.

Super caption:

'Julian Burnside still acts for the big end of town, but gives a third of his time for pro bono human-rights work.

'Josh Bornstein is now a senior partner in his firm. He continues to act for trade unions and others involved in the labour movement.'

Coombs takes the microphone. He still carries the personal legacy of the dispute in the lines of his body, the circles under his eyes, the slightly unkempt beard he has grown. It will take him some years to fully recover.

COOMBS: It's an immense honour to be given lifetime membership of the Maritime Union of Australia. And to share that honour with the bloke who was with me in the trenches ... if you'll excuse the expression – fighting doggedly every inch of the way. Greg Combet.

Super caption:

'John Coombs is leading an active retirement on his property. He is a member of the local council and remains Chairman of the Board of the MUA Superannuation Fund.'

The waterfront is the cutting edge of globalisation. It sits at the interface of global capital and labour ...

Dissolve to:

Combet and Kelty together.

KELTY: End of an era.

COMBET: Bill. Remember, you said I wasn't ready? To take over from you.

Kelty knew this was corning.

I'm ready now. And raring.

KELTY: It's going to be the toughest time in history for a union leader. This government's out to bury us.

COMBET: I know that.

Greg Combet (Daniel Frederiksen) and Bill Kelty (Francis Greenslade).

KELTY: What if I'm not ready to go?

COMBET: Power is never conceded willingly. It has to be taken.

Super caption:

'Greg Combet is now the National Secretary of the Australian Council of Trade Unions.'

Sean and Brendan are sitting having a quiet beer together.

BRENDAN: I'm getting out, mate.

SEAN: What? Why?

BRENDAN: The old man's already taken the handshake. It's changed, mate. Wearing that fuckin' blue and yellow vest every day – feels like it's strangling the life out of you. Bundying into a straddle that talks to you – 'Good morning, Brendan. Mind you don't take a piss within four hours, or management will know about it'. Blokes are already getting neck injuries from the straddle shifts. The union used to –

SEAN: ... Own the waterfront. I know. It's still there, but, mate. The union's still there ... and it nearly wasn't ...

BRENDAN: It's just my nature. I can't forgive and move on. Cherie says I've got 'anger issues'.

SEAN: What'll you do?

BRENDAN: Live off the missus, mate. Anyhow, it'll be legit soon. She's got me on the ball and chain. Wedding invitation's in the mail.

Super caption:

'Brendan Tully and Cherie Snape now run a successful machinery hire business.

'Sean McSwain returned to work on the docks, and he and Janine are expecting their third child.'

SCENE 108. INT. CORRIGAN'S OFFICE – PATRICK HEAD OFFICE. DAY.

Corrigan, Paul and Valerie at the end of a long day. Corrigan is standing by the window, staring down at the Darling Harbour docks.

Paul is running through the speech Corrigan will deliver tonight.

PAUL: Imagine the reaction if I'd stood here a year ago and said: 'This time next year, at Patrick, the nick will be gone, double headers will be gone, eight hundred of the workforce will be gone. One man, one machine ...' blah blah '... eight-hour shifts with one break, more flexible rosters and productivity bonuses linked to the number of boxes moved on a shift ... maintenance and cleaning contracted out ...' Chris, you will show a bit more interest tonight when you're actually delivering this?

CORRIGAN: (*pulling a bottle of champagne from the refrigerator*) Hmm? What? Yes, of course.

VALERIE: What are we celebrating? Have we bought an airline or something?

CORRIGAN: John Coombs' retirement. Today.

He pops the cork and pours, lifts his own glass and tilts it in the direction of Darling Harbour.

Looking west from the office, they can see a soft, Sydney, dusky pink sunset.

To Coombsie. A worthy enemy.

Super caption:

'Until recently he met John Coombs at superannuation meetings and the two often lunched together.'

Cut to black.

SCENE 109. EXT. PATRICK'S MELBOURNE DOCK. DUSK.

The sun shimmering on the water. The giant cranes silhouetted against the sunset sky.

A tiny figure stands absorbing the strange beauty of this. Then he turns and walks slowly away. It is Tony Tully. As he disappears, hold on a sticker attached to the cyclone wire of the fence: 'MUA HERE TO STAY'.

Super caption: 'The Howard Government won the 1998 election and now ranks waterfront reform as one of the successes of its first term in office.

'The non-union labourers on the docks lost their jobs and sued Chris Corrigan and the National Farmers' Federation for compensation.

'Over 90% of the Patrick waterfront staff are members of the Maritime Union.

'Having achieved a crane rate that equalled world's best practice, in April 2006 Patrick Corporation was the subject of a hostile takeover by Toll Holdings.

'Chris Corrigan is no longer with the company.'

END OF PART FOUR

Ships on the dock.

FILM END CREDITS

CAST

John Coombs
Colin Friels

Jack Thompson as
Tony Tully

Chris Corrigan
Geoff Morrell

Greg Combet
Daniel Frederiksen

Sean McSwain
Anthony Hayes

Josh Bornstein
Justin Smith

Julian Burnside
Rhys Muldoon

Brendan Tully
Daniel Wyllie

Janine McSwain
Justine Clarke

Petra Hilsen
Lucy Bell

Tali Bernard
Caroline Craig

Gwen Coombs
Deborah Kennedy

Valerie Corrigan
Helen Thomson

Derek Corrigan
Kevin Harrington

Wendy Corrigan
Liz McColl

Joseph Corrigan
Louis Corbett

Lucy Corrigan
Ashleigh Millo

Anna Combet
Joanna
Hunt-Prokhovnik

Bill Kelty
Francis Greenslade

Cherie Snape
Anna Lise Phillips

Peter Reith
Mike Bishop

Paul White
Christopher Stollery

Peter Kilfoyle
Michael Robinson

Mike Wells
Dennis Coard

Lyn Tully
Michele Fawdon

Podge
Richard Heath

Garry Coombs
Christopher Widdows

Dan Brodie
Donal Forde

Judith
Evelyn Krape

Simon
Brian Lipson

Nuts
Peter Prenga

Chopper
Russell Menzies

7:30 Report Host
Jennifer Byrne

Claude
Paul Dawber

Justice North
Denis Moore

Police Sergeant #1
Doug Bowles

Yannis
Kurtis Papadinis

Clara
Matilda Simpson

Process Server
David Tredinnick

Gary Welsh
Robert Price

Cecelia
Stephanie Capiron

Friend #1
Peter Hosking

Soldier
Daniel Diesendorf

**Soldier's
Grandmother**
Cicely Slape

Paul
Keir Saltmarsh

Reporter
Adriana Marco

**I.R.C.
Commissioner**
Rick Burchall

Frank Parry
Jeremy Kewley

Wharfie
John Teague

Security Man
Robert Plazek

Interviewer
Carolyn Bock

Mandy
Suzie Stapleton

Waitress
Megan Harrington

Barrister
Frank Bren

Justice Wilcox
John Arnold

Justice Hayne
Bruce Kerr

Justice Brennan
Kirk Alexander

Banker
Lewis Fiander

John
David Cameron

John's Wife
Jenny Barkla

Frank
Peter Lamb

Carlos
Serge Denardo

The Feral
Travis Cotton

Alex McSwain
Nicholas Mulkearns

Roger Gyles
Robert Grubb

Jenny
Niki Owen

Reporter
Adriana Marco

John Middleton
Rupert Burns

Distressed Girls
Jessica & Amy Vellucci

Maureen
Pixie Jones

Musicians
Phil Para & Lyndon Wesley

CREW

Associate Producer
Louisa Kors

Casting Director
Alison Telford

1st Assistant Director
John Powditch

Script Editor
John Alsop

ABC Production Supervisor
Greer Simpkin

ABC Business Affairs Manager
Jennifer Auzins-Barrett

Production Manager
Jenny Barty

Location Manager
Michael Gaffney

Art Director
Dale Mark

Camera Operator/Steadicam
Steve Scoble

Camera Operator
Andrew Schmidt

Focus Puller
Jem Rayner

B Focus Puller
Peter Stott

Technical Supervisor
Eric Burt

Stunt Co-ordinator
Bernie Ledger

Script Supervisor
Paul Harding

2nd Assistant Director

Darrin Oakley

Extras Casting
Martine Gow

Childrens Drama Coach
Greg Saunders

Costume Supervisor
Margot McCartney

Costume Co-ordinator
Gareth Blaha

Standby Costume
Victoria Innes

Make Up Supervisor
Ian Loughnan

Make Up Artist
Rachel Walton

Make Up and Hair Assistant
Jodie Hellingman

Sound Recordist
Colin Jones

Gavin Marsh
Boom Operator

Georgina Hanley
2nd Boom Operator

James Hardie
Key Gaffer

Michael Cleary
Tim Jones

Best Boy
Peter Holland

Key Grip
Max Gaffney

Best Boy Grip
Brian Pribble

Production Co-ordinator
Helen Boicovitis

Production Secretary
Darren McFarlane

Production Assistants
Paul Wambach

Elle Wilson
Producers Assistant

Lyla Wilson
Financial Services
Threadgold Plummer Hood

Production Accountant
Kevin Plummer

Legals
Holding Redlich
Emma Bain
Rebecca Mir

Art Dept. Co-ordinator
Jayne Russell

Buyer / Dressers
Andrew Best
Rob Molnar

Standby Props
John Santucci

Assistant Standby
Amanda Williams
Chris Greene

Unit Manager
Rick Kornaat

Catering
Editable Food

Assistant Editor
Katie Flaxman
Off-Line Edit
Island Films – Simon Dibbs

Post Production
TheLaB Sydney
– Prue Fletcher

Telecine Colourist
Annelie Chapple

Online Editor
Jo Spillane

Audio Post Production
Labsonics Australia
- Gerry Duffy

Sound Supervisor/ FX Editor
Ian Neilson

Dialogue Editor/ ADR Recording
Rick Lisle

Foley Recording
Nigel Croydon

Foley Artist
Stefan Kluka

Sound Mixer
Robert Sullivan

Completion Guarantor
Film Finances Inc

Camera Department and Production Department Attachments supported by Film Victoria

The producers would like to thank
Chris & Valerie Corrigan, Derek Corrigan, Greg Combet & Petra Hilsen, John & Gwen Coombs, Josh Bornstein & Tali Bernard, Julian Burnside, Michael O'Leary, Mike Wells, Paul White, Peter Kilfoyle, Robyn Kershaw, Roger Le Mesurier, Rebecca Anderson, Paddy Crumlin, Josephine Haussler, Zoe Reynolds, Australian Council of Trade Unions (ACTU), Maritime Union of Australia, Patrick Stevedores, Victorian Trade Union Choir, and all those organisations and individuals who kindly offered us assistance.

Produced with the assistance of Film Victoria [logo]

Developed and produced with assistance from the New South Wales Film and television office [logo]

Developed and produced in association with the Australian Broadcasting Corporation [logo]

Principal investor: Film Finance Corporation Australia [logo]